ANCHORED
in
HEALING

NAVIGATING RESILIENCE, BOUNDARIES, AND TRUST

WANDA E. NORDLIE

Dedication

*To my family, for teaching me the complexity of love,
forgiveness, and resilience. Your courage to reach out began
the healing our family truly needed, and this journey would
not have been the same without you. And to those who
have found the courage to face their truths—and to those
still searching for the strength to begin—this is for you.
May you find peace, resilience, and the power to heal.*

Contents

Introduction

Navigating Healing as a Lifelong Journey and the Power of Sharing Truth

Five years ago, when I first shared my story, I had no way of knowing the journey it would set in motion—not only for me but for countless others who saw themselves in my words. The act of opening up about my past, about secrets long hidden and wounds left to heal on their own, was both terrifying and freeing. At first, I was overwhelmed by the flood of responses: messages of support, gratitude, and even shared pain. People I had never met reached out to thank me, to share their own stories, and to express how my honesty had given them a renewed sense of courage. It was a testament to the power of truth—how speaking it aloud, even once, can create waves that ripple far beyond the initial moment.

Yet, while many of my friends and extended family embraced my decision to share, not everyone understood. My siblings, with whom I shared a complex and tangled history, reacted with anger and disappointment. Though we were adopted and had no biological ties, our shared upbringing had once forged a bond that seemed unbreakable. But in my effort to heal and find closure, I found that bond strained, the foundation of our connection shaken by my truth. This rejection was painful and, at times, bewildering. Why did my honesty, my desire to make sense of my experiences, feel like a betrayal to them? Their response forced me to confront a difficult reality: sometimes, healing demands that we step forward alone, not knowing who might follow or who may choose to turn away.

As I continued to process my own experiences and the mixed responses of my family, I began to understand that healing is never a one-time act. It is not a single revelation, nor a definitive "fix." Healing is a continuous journey, one that asks us to return to ourselves repeatedly with compassion, resilience, and a willingness to face new layers of truth as they arise. With each step, I realized that I was uncovering deeper levels of understanding—not only about myself but also about the forces that had shaped me and the ways in which I could redefine my future.

In the years that followed my first memoir, I encountered others within my extended family who reached out to share their own secrets, their own versions of the story I thought I knew. Their revelations added new dimensions to my understanding, reminding me that each of us carries pieces of a larger family narrative that only make sense when seen together. With these new insights, I was able to revisit old wounds and begin to see them with fresh eyes. This book, then, is not just about my journey but about the power of shared healing—how opening up our truths can illuminate paths for others and bring us closer to a collective understanding.

In these chapters, I hope to share what I have learned about resilience, forgiveness, boundaries, and trust. Each page represents a facet of the journey I have been on, a journey that has taught me that healing is as much about the present as it is about the past. This book is a testament to the ways we can reclaim our power, redefine our identities, and build lives that are rooted in authenticity and purpose.

Whether you are grappling with your own family history, confronting painful truths, or simply seeking to live a life that feels true to who you are, I hope this book offers you solace, guidance, and encouragement. Healing is not always easy, but it is always possible. In sharing my story, I hope to offer you a light along the path—a reminder that you are not alone, and that each step forward brings you closer to a place of peace.

CHAPTER 1

Anchoring the Journey: The Path to Continued Healing

When I decided to publish my memoir, I felt both free and terrified. I was offering my story to the world, a story that held more than my pain—it held secrets that had lingered in the shadows for decades. Would I be seen as courageous, or would there be feelings of betrayal by the revelations that, for me, had been a pathway to healing? As messages of gratitude and connection poured in from strangers, my heart swelled with purpose. Yet, within my own family, there was a shadow of resistance. My siblings, our bond forged by shared experiences, were unable to reconcile with the truths I had revealed.

This emotional divergence became a new chapter in my healing. Letters from strangers reminded me why I spoke out, while family silence tested my resolve. I began to learn that healing comes not only from sharing but from navigating the emotional terrain that truth can unearth. Each message I received reminded me of the power of courage, even when it costs us. People shared their gratitude, expressing that they felt seen, understood, and somehow less alone. Many conveyed that my memoir echoed their own, that they, too, carried secrets burdened with pain and silence. They wrote about how my words had given them hope—a validation of their struggles and a reminder that healing, though difficult, was possible. My heart swelled as I read each letter, yet there was a shadow cast across the warmth, a whisper of fear that grew louder with each day.

The truth, though freeing for me, had unsettled others. My siblings, each of us bound not by blood but by shared history, turned their backs on me. We had been through everything together—or so I had thought. We shared an unspoken understanding of what lay beneath the surface of our family's history, an acknowledgment of the things we had each endured. But my memoir threatened that understanding, unraveling the threads that held us together. While the world outside was responding with compassion, my family's response struck with the force of wounds freshly reopened.

For the first time, I saw the consequences of my courage through their eyes. I could almost hear them accusing me of dredging up the past for attention, of casting our family's image in a shadow that could never be lifted. Yet the truth was never about shaming them. It was about claiming my story, a story that had festered in silence for far too long. But their rejection felt like a price I had not anticipated paying. I found myself questioning the very journey I had taken, wondering if sharing my truth had been a mistake.

That questioning, that doubt, lasted only so long as the next message from a stranger would arrive, offering a reminder of why I had chosen to speak out. One letter stood out among them all, written by a cousin who, like me, had endured in silence. They thanked me not only for my bravery but for validating experiences they, too, had tried to bury. The words in their letter felt like a balm, healing the fresh wounds of rejection. I realized that by stepping into my truth, I had inadvertently opened doors for others to confront their own stories, to make peace with their pasts.

This experience taught me that courage, while empowering, often comes with consequences. But it also revealed that courage can be contagious, spreading to those who might have been silent forever had it not been for someone else taking the first step. This ripple effect of truth-telling offered a sense of purpose I had not anticipated. In a way, the memoir had become more than just my story—it had become a gateway for others to find their voices.

Key Takeaways for Readers

1. **Embracing the Consequences of Truth**: Sharing personal truths can evoke unexpected reactions; it is essential to hold space for both validation and rejection. Know that this is common and can be part of the journey toward healing. Accepting that not everyone will support or understand you is vital in building resilience.

2. **Finding Strength in Unexpected Places**: Support often comes from unexpected places— remain open to these connections. Keep an open heart to new connections and unexpected allies, as these individuals can offer validation that helps counterbalance the rejection of others.

3. **Courage Is Contagious**: Courage may disrupt old dynamics but can plant seeds for broader healing. Remember that your bravery has the power to inspire others. By speaking up, you might be opening doors for others to confront their past, to heal, and to forgive.

The revelation of family secrets and the ensuing journey of navigating public and private reactions taught me many things about resilience. As supportive as my extended family and strangers had been, their encouragement alone could not fully shield me from the complex emotions that arose from my siblings' rejection. Each strained relationship, each silence or sharp response, weighed on me in a way that words from others could not easily counterbalance. But this process of sharing and facing backlash also revealed to me that healing required a resilience I had not fully appreciated before.

In the quiet moments, when the noise of responses faded and I was alone with my thoughts, I found myself wrestling with self-doubt. Was sharing the truth worth the pain it had caused? In confronting these feelings, I came to understand that resilience is not a trait we inherit or simply possess—it is something we cultivate. Like a muscle, it grows stronger through use, and with each challenge, I found myself more equipped to withstand the emotional storms that followed.

One aspect of resilience I found especially challenging was recognizing the need to stand firm in my truth without constantly justifying myself to others. My siblings' reactions had triggered a powerful instinct in me to explain, to defend my choices, and to clarify my intentions. I wanted them to understand that my memoir was not shared out of malice or to cast a shadow over them, but to help myself heal and to inspire others to confront their own pasts. Yet, as time passed, I realized that continually seeking validation or understanding from them was exhausting and a futile endeavor. In that realization, I found a new layer of resilience—the strength to let go of the need for approval from those who might never offer it.

As I let go of this need, I also discovered a deeper resilience in my own self-acceptance. I reminded myself that I had chosen this path of healing and truth because it aligned with my deepest values, not because I sought anyone's approval. This shift was freeing. No longer feeling compelled to explain myself, I began to experience a peace I had not known before, a sense of wholeness that came from standing firm in my story and embracing the reality that some relationships might remain fractured indefinitely.

Over time, I also learned that resilience could be nurtured through small acts of self-care and community building. Surrounding myself with supportive people— friends, mentors, and even therapists—who validated my experience allowed me to anchor myself during moments of loneliness and rejection. I leaned into the support they offered, finding strength in their words and encouragement. They reminded me that my journey was not a solitary one; it was part of a larger, interconnected tapestry of resilience, shared by others who had also faced difficult truths within their families.

Through this, I realized that resilience, much like courage, is contagious. Each person who supported me became part of a circle of strength, one that kept growing as others entered the fold. It became evident that while I had felt alone initially, I was, in fact, surrounded by an invisible network of resilience—one that I had unknowingly built through sharing my truth.

Practical Steps for Building Resilience

1. **Embrace the Process of Letting Go**: Releasing the need for others' approval can be challenging, especially when they are close family members. Start with small steps, like reframing interactions and acknowledging that your journey is yours alone.

2. **Create a Circle of Support**: Surround yourself with people who validate and encourage you, whether that's friends, supportive family members, or professionals like therapists. Your circle of support is a crucial foundation for resilience.

3. **Practice Self-Care and Grounding**: Engaging in simple self-care practices, such as journaling, meditation, or regular physical activity, helps anchor your resilience. These practices provide emotional stability during challenging times.

In reflecting on the impact of sharing my memoir, I began to see that the process was not just about the act of disclosure—it was about the slow, transformative journey that followed. Each time I revisited my memories, I found myself peeling back yet another layer of understanding, examining the emotions that lay hidden beneath the initial shock and liberation of sharing. I came to realize that healing was not a destination but a continuous process, requiring me to re-approach my past with patience and a willingness to see things from new perspectives.

One such shift in perspective came when I thought about my siblings' reactions. While their rejection had initially struck me as a profound loss, I began to see it through a different lens. Their response was less about me and more about their struggle to confront truths that they were not ready to face. This realization did not erase the hurt I felt, but it allowed me to step back and hold compassion for them in a way I had not been able to before. It reminded me that healing often involves forgiving others, not necessarily for their benefit, but for our own peace and growth.

This compassion, however, did not mean accepting unhealthy behavior. Instead, it guided me toward setting healthy boundaries that allowed me to protect my well-being without closing myself off entirely. I learned that compassion and boundaries could coexist—that I could wish my siblings peace and understanding while also choosing not to engage in dynamics that drained me. This balancing act became a core part of my resilience, teaching me that I could hold space for my own growth without feeling guilty for letting go of connections that no longer served my journey.

Interestingly, as I embraced this balance of compassion and boundaries, I noticed shifts in some of my relationships. Certain family members, whom I initially believed would never understand my decision to share my memoir, started to reach out with quiet support. They would send brief messages, just a line or two, but each one felt like a small step toward bridging the gap that had formed. It was as if, in holding true to my boundaries and cultivating resilience, I was indirectly inviting others to reconsider their stance, allowing them to approach the truth at their own pace.

This delicate dance of connection and distance became a crucial lesson in trust. I learned to trust that healing would unfold not only in myself but potentially in those around me, too, though perhaps not on my timeline. There was a kind of freedom in relinquishing control over how others responded to my memoir. Trusting in the process meant allowing each relationship to take its natural course, without forcing or expecting certain outcomes. It was a trust born not from naive hope, but from an understanding that each of us has our own path to walk.

In embracing this mindset, I found a renewed sense of purpose in my journey. My memoir, once a personal burden, had become a tool for connection and growth—both for me and for others. I began to see that healing was a collective experience, shared through small acts of courage, compassion, and resilience that rippled outward, touching lives in ways I could never fully know or control.

This realization brought a peace that settled deep within me, a quiet knowing that sharing my truth, while difficult, had been the right choice.

Key Insights on Healing Through Boundaries and Compassion

1. **Boundaries Are a Form of Compassion**: Setting boundaries does not mean closing yourself off. Boundaries allow you to maintain healthy relationships without sacrificing your well-being.

2. **Allowing Others to Process in Their Own Time**: Remember that others may need time to confront their own feelings about your truth. Give space for this, knowing that each individual's journey unfolds uniquely.

3. **Trust the Process of Healing**: Healing is not always immediate, nor is it linear. Trust that growth is happening, even when it is not visible or happening in the way you expected.

In the weeks and months following the release of my memoir, I started to recognize that healing was not something I could experience in isolation. My journey had touched others—family, friends, even strangers—and their responses created a complex web of relationships that I had to navigate carefully. It was as if my memoir had spilled over into the lives of those around me, forcing them to confront not only my truth but also aspects of themselves they might have kept hidden.

One of the most profound lessons I learned during this time was about shared vulnerability. Through letters and conversations, I came to understand that many of those who reached out to me were drawn by a need to find someone who understood their pain, even if it was only through words on a page. They, too, were carrying wounds—some as fresh as mine, others as old as the memories they could barely speak of. My memoir became a mirror for them, reflecting fragments of their own lives and struggles.

This realization was humbling. I saw that by opening up, I had inadvertently given others permission to acknowledge their own stories. Some of my extended family members, particularly my cousins, wrote to me with gratitude, sharing their own painful experiences and thanking me for breaking the silence that had loomed over our family for so long. They told me how, in reading my words, they felt seen and validated. For the first time, they could face parts of their past they had been unable to look at before.

But with this shared vulnerability came a sense of responsibility. It became clear that healing was not just about addressing my own experiences; it was also about holding space for others as they began to confront their truths. I realized that my memoir had woven itself into a broader tapestry, one where each person's healing contributed to a collective sense of resilience and understanding.

Yet, there was a delicate balance to maintain. While I wanted to support others in their healing journeys, I also knew I had to protect my own emotional well-being. I learned that I could not carry their stories on my shoulders, that each person had to walk their own path toward healing. This was a challenging truth to accept, especially when faced with the weight of their shared pain, but it was necessary. Just as I had come to understand the importance of boundaries with my siblings, I realized I needed to set similar boundaries with those who reached out for comfort.

In creating these boundaries, I was able to connect with others more authentically. I could offer empathy without becoming overwhelmed, support without becoming enmeshed in their experiences. This approach allowed me to stay grounded in my own healing journey while still being there for others in a meaningful way. It was a lesson in balance, one that taught me the value of giving from a place of strength rather than sacrifice.

As I continued to process the impact of my memoir, I felt a growing sense of peace in knowing that my journey was no longer just mine alone. My courage had sparked a movement within my family and my community, one where others could find solace in their own vulnerability. This understanding brought me to a place of acceptance, allowing me to honor my story while respecting the healing journeys of others.

Advice on Navigating Shared Vulnerability

1. **Allow Space for Others Without Absorbing Their Pain**: Support those who reach out but remember that each person's journey is their own. Offer empathy, but do not take on emotional burdens that are not yours to carry.

2. **Set Boundaries in Emotional Connections**: Setting boundaries does not mean closing yourself off; it means preserving your energy so you can offer support without sacrificing your well-being.

3. **Acknowledge the Collective Power of Healing**: Your story is part of a larger journey. Embrace the shared resilience and understanding that comes when we open up and support each other's healing.

As I navigated these initial stages of sharing my memoir and connecting with others who had been impacted by my words, I discovered that healing was not as straightforward as I had once believed. Just when I thought I had reached a place of peace, another layer of emotions would surface, reminding me that healing is cyclical rather than linear. Each new conversation, each story shared with me by family or strangers, unearthed feelings I had to revisit, reprocess, and release.

One of the most challenging aspects of this journey was learning to accept the shifting dynamics in relationships that I had once thought unbreakable. Family, once a term that evoked feelings of safety and unity, now held a different meaning. My relationships with some cousins, strengthened by a shared understanding, had grown deeper, while others remained distant, their silence a reminder of the differing ways we each responded to trauma. These complexities taught me that healing sometimes means redefining what family looks like and accepting that some relationships may not survive the weight of truth.

In these moments, I leaned heavily on self-compassion. Whenever a memory or a painful feeling resurfaced, I reminded myself that it was natural to feel both peace and pain on this journey. Self-compassion became a lifeline, allowing me to honor each emotion without rushing to "fix" it. I realized that my worth was not diminished by the times I struggled. Rather, it was in facing these struggles that I found strength. Every moment of self-compassion brought me closer to the resilience needed to continue this path.

Alongside self-compassion, I discovered the necessity of grounding myself in the present. The weight of the past can be overwhelming, especially when revisiting traumatic memories, and grounding practices helped me find balance. Simple techniques like deep breathing, journaling, and taking mindful walks allowed me to remain connected to the present, rather than being swept away by the intensity of my past. These practices became essential tools, offering me stability and a sense of control in moments when emotions felt overwhelming.

As I continued to engage with others' stories and support them in their own healing, I found myself questioning what it truly meant to "heal." I realized that healing was not a single destination to be reached but a journey with countless stops along the way. It involved accepting every part of myself—the parts that were still hurt, the parts that had healed, and the parts that continued to transform with each new experience. Healing, I learned, was an ongoing dialogue with myself, one that required patience, acceptance, and, most importantly, love.

This page in my journey reaffirmed that courage was not about erasing the scars of the past but rather learning to carry them with grace. I began to see my experiences as chapters in a larger story, each one adding depth to who I am today. And through this journey, I hoped to offer others the reminder that they, too, could find peace—not by hiding their scars but by embracing them as evidence of the resilience that had brought them through.

Reflections for Embracing a Nonlinear Healing Journey

1. **Embrace Each Emotion as It Arises**: Healing is not a straight line. Accept each emotion, even those that contradict each other, as part of the journey toward wholeness.

2. **Practice Grounding to Stay in the Present**: Use grounding techniques to remain anchored in the present, especially when difficult memories surface. This helps you find balance amid emotional waves.

3. **Redefine What Healing Means to You**: Healing is a personal journey that does not need to conform to anyone else's expectations. Define it on your own terms, allowing space for both growth and setbacks.

CHAPTER 2

Navigating Resilience After Disclosure

When I first decided to share my memoir, I knew that some of my family might struggle to accept it. But I had not fully prepared myself for the emotional landscape that would unfold once the book was published. It was one thing to speak the truth in private, to release years of silence into my own journal or in therapy sessions. It was quite another way to open that truth to the world, allowing my experiences to be seen, heard, and, inevitably, judged. As much as I had anticipated mixed reactions, the reality was more painful than I could have imagined.

The initial rejection from my siblings hit me hardest. We were not biologically connected, but our shared experiences had always made them feel like my closest family. Or so I had thought. Their reaction felt like a severing of a bond I had always taken for granted, a withdrawal of support that left me feeling more exposed than I had been when I had written the book. At first, I wanted to reach out to them, to explain myself, to somehow bridge the chasm that had formed between us. But each attempt to connect felt like pushing against a locked door. They were not ready to understand, or maybe they just did not want to. In any case, I had to accept that their journey to understanding was not something I could control.

Sitting with the pain of their rejection was a challenge I had not anticipated. The hurt ran deep, touching wounds that I thought had long since healed. It felt as though my past, the traumas I had struggled to overcome, were being judged all over again—not just by society, but by the people I had thought would support me the most. My siblings' reactions became a test of resilience, forcing me to dig into the strength I had built over years of therapy and introspection. I reminded myself that I had chosen this path not for anyone else's validation, but because telling my story had been essential to my healing.

In processing these reactions, I began to confront a hard truth: not everyone will understand or accept our personal journeys, and sometimes, those closest to us are the ones who resist the most. This realization was painful, but it was also freeing. It allowed me to begin releasing the need for their approval. I saw that holding onto that need only kept me tethered to expectations I could never meet. By letting go, I began reclaiming my story, accepting that my truth was valid even if it made others uncomfortable.

As I navigated these feelings, I found that one of the most powerful tools for resilience was self-compassion. Each time self-doubt crept in, or when memories of my siblings' rejection resurfaced, I reminded myself that my feelings were valid. I was not weak for being hurt; I was human. Practicing self-compassion helped me to honor my pain without letting it consume me. It allowed me to approach my emotions with gentleness, treating myself with the same kindness I would offer a friend going through a similar experience.

In these moments of self-compassion, I also began to reflect on identity—on who I was, not just as a sibling, but as an individual with a unique story and voice. I realized that my identity did not have to be defined by my family's perception of me. I had my own values, my own perspective, and my own truth, all of which were valid, regardless of who did or did not approve. This shift in perspective allowed me to see myself more clearly, separate from the roles I had played within my family. I was more than a sibling or a member of a family; I was someone who had survived, who had healed, and who had found the courage to share that journey with the world.

Practical Steps for Navigating Family Rejection

1. **Release the Need for Approval**: Acknowledge that not everyone will understand your journey. Release the need for their approval, knowing that your path to healing is yours alone.

2. **Practice Self-Compassion**: When family reactions bring up feelings of hurt or self-doubt, approach these emotions with gentleness. Remind yourself that your feelings are valid and give yourself permission to feel and process them.

3. **Redefine Your Identity Outside of Family Roles**: Reflect on who you are beyond the roles assigned within your family. Embrace your unique story, values, and perspective, allowing yourself to stand in your truth without seeking validation.

As time passed, I began to notice subtle shifts in my own reactions to the silence and resistance I encountered from family. Initially, the absence of support from my siblings and the awkwardness with extended family felt overwhelming, like a void that could not be filled. But slowly, I began to make peace with the reality that some relationships might never be the same. There was both sadness and a strange relief in this acceptance. Letting go of expectations for how others should respond became a way of unburdening myself, a release of the weight I had unknowingly carried for so long.

In learning to let go, I discovered an important distinction: forgiving others does not always mean inviting them back into my life. I could hold compassion for my siblings, even as I accepted that our connection might be irrevocably altered. This realization was freeing. It allowed me to maintain a sense of inner peace without feeling the need to continually defend my choices or seek their approval. It was an acceptance that forgiveness and boundaries could coexist, each reinforcing the other.

The more I embraced this balance, the more I saw that boundaries were essential for my emotional well-being. Without them, I would have been constantly tethered to the highs and lows of others' reactions, my self-worth rising and falling with each word or silence. But by defining my own limits, I created a safe space for healing—a place where my story could exist on its own terms, unshaken by the judgment or approval of others. This boundary was not a wall; it was a sanctuary, a place of strength where I could continue my journey without interference.

This shift in perspective was not easy. At times, I struggled with guilt, wondering if setting boundaries was somehow selfish or unkind. But I soon learned that boundaries are not about closing others out; they are about allowing myself to heal without distraction or external expectations.

I reminded myself that just as my story was mine alone to tell, my healing journey was also uniquely my own. No one else had to understand or approve of it for it to be valid.

During this time, I leaned on a close circle of friends and supportive family members who helped me stay grounded. They reminded me of the strength it had taken to share my story in the first place, and they validated the importance of protecting my journey. Their presence was a comforting reminder that I was not alone, that even if some relationships had changed, I still had a network of support that believed in my healing.

Reflecting on these experiences, I came to understand that resilience was not just about enduring pain—it was about finding ways to thrive, even amid uncertainty and change. It meant creating an environment where I could continue to grow, even if certain people could no longer be part of that growth. Each boundary I set, each expectation I released, was a step toward cultivating a life that honored my truth and allowed me the freedom to heal on my own terms.

Practical Strategies for Setting Boundaries in Family Relationships

1. **Define Your Emotional Boundaries**: Identify what interactions leave you feeling drained or unsettled and give yourself permission to limit these without guilt. Boundaries protect your peace.

2. **Allow Space for Compassion Without Compromise**: You can hold compassion for others without sacrificing your own well-being. Recognize that forgiveness does not require continued closeness.

3. **Build a Supportive Circle Outside of Family Dynamics**: Lean on friends, mentors, or therapists who respect your journey and offer encouragement. Having this support network strengthens your resilience.

As I deepened my understanding of boundaries, they served not only as a form of protection but as an affirmation of my commitment to healing. Boundaries reminded me that my well-being mattered, and I could choose what felt safe and nurturing. While I had once seen boundaries as a last resort, something to be used only when all else failed, I now embraced them as a fundamental part of self-respect. They became my way of saying, "I value my peace, my journey, and my right to heal on my own terms."

This shift was not always easy to explain, especially to family members who were accustomed to a different version of me—one who had often prioritized harmony over honesty, one who avoided conflict to keep the peace. In stepping into this new approach, I encountered resistance not only from others but within myself. Part of me wondered if I was being too harsh if setting boundaries meant abandoning the values of family loyalty and forgiveness that I had grown up with. It took time, patience, and introspection to reconcile these conflicting beliefs.

Through this inner work, I came to a powerful realization: boundaries and love can coexist. Holding boundaries with those who have hurt me does not mean I care for them any less. In fact, it means that I care for myself enough to protect my energy and that I care for them enough to want our interactions to be healthy and respectful. Boundaries, I discovered, can be an act of love—not the romanticized, self-sacrificing love that often appears in family dynamics, but a mature love that respects the autonomy of all involved.

This understanding began to transform my relationships. Where there was once an invisible line of resentment and obligation, I started building genuine connections based on mutual respect and understanding. Family members who valued this new approach began to respond differently, respecting the space I created and meeting me in a place of honesty. Others, however, remained distant, unable, or unwilling to adjust to the new dynamics. And that was okay.

I learned to release the need for everyone's approval and focused instead on nurturing relationships that honored my journey.

One of the most surprising aspects of this transformation was the sense of peace that came with letting go of certain expectations. In giving up the idea that everyone in my family had to understand or support me, I freed myself from the cycle of disappointment and frustration. I accepted that each person's capacity for understanding is shaped by their own experiences and that I could not change those perspectives. What I could change, however, was my response. Instead of seeking validation from those who might never give it, I grounded myself in the affirmation that my journey was valid simply because it was mine.

In this new mindset, I found profound freedom. I could still love my family, appreciate the good memories, and acknowledge their impact on my life without feeling bound to the expectations they held. By letting go of the need for their understanding, I allowed myself to fully inhabit my own story, to live in a way that felt true to who I was becoming. This freedom was like a breath of fresh air, a reminder that I was allowed to grow beyond the limits that others might set for me.

Key Lessons in Balancing Boundaries and Family Loyalty

1. **Boundaries Can Be an Act of Love**: Setting limits does not mean closing off love. Instead, it allows you to maintain healthy interactions that respect your well-being.

2. **Release the Need for Universal Approval**: Accept that not everyone in your family will understand or support your journey. Embrace the freedom that comes with living authentically, regardless of others' opinions.

3. **Focus on Relationships That Respect Your Growth**: Invest in relationships that honor your healing and growth. This allows you to nurture connections based on mutual respect, rather than outdated expectations.

As I continued to explore the boundaries I had set, I began to appreciate just how much they allowed me to regain control over my own story. In stepping back from certain family dynamics, I found that I could reclaim my narrative, defining who I was on my own terms rather than through the roles I had been assigned by others. Each boundary I held became a testament to my commitment to healing, a way of saying to myself that I deserved peace and integrity.

This newfound perspective led me to another powerful realization: I did not need to be the person my family remembered. For so long, I had allowed their memories, their perceptions, and their expectations to shape how I saw myself. But the truth was that I had grown, changed, and transformed in ways they might never fully understand. Holding onto their version of me was like wearing a jacket that no longer fit—restricting and uncomfortable, a reminder of a past self that no longer existed.

As I released these old versions of myself, I also released the weight of trying to manage their expectations. I had always wanted my family to see me for who I truly was, but I realized that I could live in my truth without needing them to acknowledge it. In this acceptance, I found a surprising strength—a confidence in knowing that I could be myself even if they did not understand. I was not defined by their approval, nor did my worth depend on their acceptance.

Reclaiming my narrative was not an easy process, though. There were days when I questioned my choices, wondering if I was being selfish or insensitive. These were people who had shaped my early life, who had shared in my memories and milestones. But as I reminded myself, honoring my journey did not mean disregarding those connections. Instead, it meant redefining them in a way that respected both my growth and theirs. By setting boundaries, I was not pushing them away; I was creating a space where I could thrive without compromising my values.

Over time, I noticed that some family members began to shift their perspectives. Perhaps seeing me stand firm in my truth encouraged them to reexamine their own beliefs about family and forgiveness. Small gestures—a supportive message, an unexpected phone call—hinted that they were beginning to understand, if only a little. And though these moments of connection were few, they served as reminders that growth is possible even in relationships that seem stagnant.

These small changes reinforced for me the value of staying true to my journey, even when it felt lonely or misunderstood. I realized that I did not have to explain myself to be understood; my actions spoke for themselves. Living with integrity became my silent message, a testament to the strength I had found within. And though I might not have had everyone's support, I knew that I was enough— that my journey, my story, and my healing were valid, even if I walked this path alone.

Reflections on Reclaiming Your Narrative

1. **Release Old Versions of Yourself**: Accept that you have grown and evolved beyond the role's family members may remember. Let go of outdated expectations to live authentically.

2. **Trust in the Power of Integrity**: Living in alignment with your values sends a powerful

message. You do not have to explain yourself for others to understand.

3. **Recognize Growth, Even in Small Moments:** Stay open to small signs of understanding or connection from family members. These moments, though rare, can serve as reminders of the value of staying true to yourself.

Reflecting on this journey of navigating family reactions, I came to understand that healing from shared history requires a balance of both acceptance and release. I could acknowledge the role my family played in my past, honoring the memories and connections that shaped me, while still allowing myself the freedom to grow beyond them. It was like tending a garden—some parts could be cherished and kept, while others needed to be pruned to make room for new growth. Learning to hold both gratitude and detachment felt like an art, one that required patience and resilience.

This balance also taught me the importance of self-validation. With each step I took away from old expectations, I found myself relying less on the approval of others. Instead, I began to build my own sense of worth from within. This shift was not about rejecting my family or denying their influence but rather about recognizing that my journey was my own. I had the right to validate my experiences, my growth, and my healing without needing anyone else's endorsement.

As I continued to lean into self-validation, I noticed a profound change in my inner dialogue. I was no longer looking for others to affirm that I was on the right path; I could sense it in the peace I felt and in the confidence that grew as I honored my boundaries. This inner shift made it easier to handle moments when family members questioned my decisions or seemed unable to understand my journey. I no longer felt compelled to explain or defend myself; my story did not need justification to be valid.

In reclaiming this power of self-validation, I found a new sense of empowerment. I began to see that I could carry my past with dignity, embracing my story fully while letting go of the need to be understood by everyone. This empowerment was not rooted in defiance but in quiet self-assurance, an understanding that my worth was inherent and unshaken by external opinions. This acceptance of my own journey allowed me to walk forward with confidence, embracing the unknown with open arms.

The process of embracing my story without seeking others' approval was transformative. It allowed me to build a foundation of self-trust, a deep belief in my ability to heal and grow, regardless of how others perceived my choices. This self-trust became my anchor, reminding me I could weather any storm if I stayed true to my values and path.

As I continue this path, I hold onto the lessons I learned from these experiences. I know now that my journey may never be fully understood by those around me, and that is okay. My healing, my story, and my truth are enough, not because they are accepted by others, but because they are a testament to my resilience. In releasing the need for approval, I have found a freedom that allows me to live authentically, honoring my past while fully embracing the possibilities of the future.

Empowering Practices for Self-Validation

1. **Cultivate Self-Validation**: Build a habit of affirming your own experiences and choices. Acknowledge that your journey is valid because it is yours, not because others approve.

2. **Practice Self-Trust as Your Anchor**: Develop self-trust by aligning your actions with your values. This trust will ground you, offering stability even when others question your path.

3. **Embrace the Art of Balance in Family Dynamics**: Hold onto cherished memories but give yourself permission to grow beyond past roles. Balancing gratitude and detachment are key to moving forward.

CHAPTER 3

Anchoring Forgiveness: Finding Freedom Through Letting Go

When I shared my story, I expected a mixture of reactions— support from some, skepticism from others, and some lingering silence from family members who were not ready to confront the past. What I had not anticipated, though, was the cascade of new revelations that would follow. The release of my memoir acted like a key that unlocked other stories, memories, and secrets that had long been buried. Suddenly, family members I had not spoken to in years— particularly some of my cousins—were reaching out to share their own experiences, pieces of a larger puzzle that I had not fully seen before.

The stories they shared were both affirming and heartbreaking. They spoke of experiences like mine, recounting moments of silence, confusion, and pain shadowing their lives. Their words were like echoes of my own, reminders that I was not alone in facing these hidden truths. For so long, I had thought of my story as uniquely mine, a solitary journey through a history that felt isolating. But now, as my cousins shared their stories, I began to see how interconnected our experiences truly were. We had all been affected by the same undercurrents, the same unspoken realities that had shaped our family.

These revelations brought a complex mix of emotions. On the one hand, there was a sense of solidarity, a comfort in knowing that my story was part of a collective experience. But there was also a new layer of grief. Hearing their stories brought feelings of sadness and empathy for the struggles they had endured in silence. I realized that while I had found a degree of healing through sharing my journey, many of my family members were still grappling with their own truths, hesitant to break the silence that had bound them for so long.

As each story unfolded, I felt the weight of this shared pain, but also the resilience that had brought each of us to this moment of honesty. In sharing their experiences, my cousins allowed me to see our family in a new light. I began to understand that my journey was not just about my own healing; it was part of a larger movement within our family, a ripple effect that encouraged others to confront their own stories. This collective unfolding brought a depth to my healing that I had not expected—a reminder that our paths, while unique, were woven together by the same threads of courage and vulnerability.

Navigating these new revelations required me to find a delicate balance between empathy and self-preservation. Each story brought with it an emotional weight, a reminder of wounds that had yet to fully heal. I wanted to be there for my family, to listen and offer support, but I also knew that I had to protect my own heart. Learning to hold space for their stories without absorbing their pain became essential. It was a practice of compassionate detachment, allowing me to honor their experiences while staying grounded in my own journey.

In listening to their stories, I realized that healing was not a solitary act; it was a shared process, one that created connections even in moments of pain. My family and I might never fully understand each other's paths, but through these conversations, we found a shared language of resilience. We began to see that our struggles, while different, were rooted in the same history—a history that had shaped us all in ways we were only beginning to understand.

Guidelines for Navigating New Family Revelations

1. **Practice Compassionate Listening**: When family members share their experiences, listen without judgment or advice. Offer empathy but remember that you are not responsible for their healing.

2. **Set Boundaries to Protect Your Heart**: While it is important to support loved ones, it is equally important to maintain boundaries that allow you to stay grounded in your own healing.

3. **Recognize the Power of Collective Healing**: Embrace the shared strength that comes from hearing each other's stories. Acknowledge that healing can be a collective journey, enriching your own path.

As more of my cousins came forward with their own stories, I found myself both overwhelmed and deeply moved. Each conversation felt like another piece of a puzzle I had not known existed. While I had spent years trying to make sense of my own experiences, it became clear that my story was only one strand in a much larger tapestry of family secrets and struggles. Their stories filled in gaps, offering perspectives I had not considered, and revealing how our shared history had impacted us in unusual ways.

One cousin, in particular, shared memories that mirrored my own so closely it was as if we had lived parallel lives, each carrying similar burdens in silence. Hearing their story was like looking into a mirror, reflecting the emotions I had held alone for so long. There was a strange comfort in knowing that the pain I had experienced was not mine alone; it was woven into the fabric of our family, passed down through generations. This realization brought with it a bittersweet sense of connection—a reminder of the ties that bound us, even in our individual pain.

Yet, as each new story unfolded, I began to feel the weight of these revelations. I wanted to honor their courage in sharing, to hold space for their truths, but I also felt the need to protect my own journey. The stories they shared were powerful, stirring memories and emotions within me that I had carefully worked to process over the years. It became clear that, while our paths were interconnected, each of us had to face our own truths in our own time. My role, I realized, was not to carry their stories for them, but to bear witness—to listen, to empathize, and to let go.

This process of bearing witness, of being present without absorbing, required me to develop a new kind of resilience. I had to find ways to hold space for my cousins without letting their pain reopen old wounds within me. It was a lesson in boundaries and compassion, a practice of remaining grounded even as I offered support. I learned to breathe through moments of discomfort, to remind myself that I could be both empathetic and protective of my own heart.

As I navigated these interactions, I noticed how these revelations affected my own healing journey. Each story brought a new perspective, a piece of the puzzle that deepened my understanding of our family's history. This unfolding of truths allowed me to reframe my own experiences, to see them as part of a shared legacy rather than isolated events. It was a strange yet powerful realization—that healing could come not only from within but from understanding the collective wounds we carried as a family.

In embracing this collective aspect of healing, I felt a renewed sense of purpose. My journey was no longer about finding peace for myself; it was about honoring the courage of those who had shared their stories with me. Together, we were uncovering layers of truth that had long been hidden, allowing ourselves to be seen, not just by each other, but by our own hearts. In this shared vulnerability, I found strength—a reminder that healing, while deeply personal, could also be a bridge that connected us.

Reflections on Shared Healing and Personal Boundaries

1. **Bear Witness Without Absorbing Pain**: When listening to others' stories, remind yourself that you can offer empathy without internalizing their experiences. Holding space does not require you to take on their emotional burdens.

2. **Embrace the Power of Collective Understanding**: Recognize that healing can deepen when we see our experiences as part of a larger family narrative. This shared understanding can bring comfort and perspective.

3. **Protect Your Own Heart Through Boundaries**: Setting limits with loved ones is essential for staying grounded in your own journey. Allow yourself to care for others without compromising your own healing.

As I continued to reflect on the stories my cousins shared, I began to realize that each revelation, each piece of our family's history, was helping me to reframe my own understanding of the past. The secrets that had once seemed like isolated events were part of a larger narrative, one that had influenced each generation in ways we had not fully understood. This awareness brought a kind of clarity, a new lens through which I could view not only my own journey but the choices and behaviors of those around me.

This deeper understanding allowed me to hold compassion for family members in ways I had not anticipated. In the past, I had felt anger or resentment toward certain individuals, unable to reconcile their actions with the pain I had experienced. But hearing about the experiences of my cousins helped me see that many of us had been affected by similar traumas, each shaped in unusual ways by the same history of silence. This realization did not erase the hurt, but it did allow me to soften, to recognize that each of us had been navigating our own struggles with limited tools and understanding.

Holding compassion in this way did not mean excusing past actions; rather, it meant acknowledging the complexity of our shared history. It was a way of saying, "I see you, and I understand that your actions were shaped by circumstances beyond either of our control." This perspective brought a surprising sense of peace. By releasing the need to hold anyone accountable for the entire weight of our family's history, I found myself more able to focus on my own healing, unburdened by old resentments.

In exploring this new compassion, I also encountered a profound sense of responsibility. With each story that was shared, I became increasingly aware of the need to break the cycle of silence that had persisted for generations. I did not want future members of our family to feel the isolation or confusion that had marked so much of our experience. By bringing these stories to light, I was contributing to a legacy of honesty, one that could offer future generations the chance to navigate their own lives with a clearer understanding of where they came from.

Yet, I was also mindful of the boundaries I needed to maintain. While I wanted to be present for my family, I recognized that I could not carry their healing for them. Each of us had to walk our own path, and while our stories intersected, our journeys were our own. This realization reinforced the importance of compassionate boundaries, a way of caring for my family without sacrificing my own well-being. It was a delicate balance, one that required constant mindfulness and self-reflection.

As I continued this path, I found strength in knowing that each story shared was a step toward collective healing. Together, we were rewriting our family's narrative, transforming a history of silence into one of openness and resilience. This shift felt powerful, a reminder that even in the face of painful truths, we could choose a new way forward. It was a journey not only of individual healing but of creating a new legacy—one rooted in honesty, compassion, and the courage to face the past together.

Practices for Honoring Family History
Without Carrying Its Weight

1. **Acknowledge the Complexity of Shared History**: Recognize that family dynamics are often shaped by generations of experiences. Hold compassion without excusing harmful actions, allowing yourself to release resentment. Forgiveness is a gift to yourself, not a validation of others' actions.

2. **Contribute to a Legacy of Honesty**: Embrace your role in transforming family narratives. By speaking openly, you can offer future generations a path to understanding and resilience.

3. **Maintain Compassionate Boundaries**: Balance empathy with self-care. Support family members in their healing without taking on their emotional burdens.

As I continued to listen to my cousins' stories and reflect on our shared past, I felt the beginning of a shift in my understanding of family loyalty. Growing up, loyalty was often defined by silence—a quiet agreement to keep family matters within the walls of our homes, no matter the cost. Breaking that silence was seen as a betrayal, a violation of unspoken rules that had been handed down through generations. But as more family members opened up, I began to see loyalty in a different light. Rather than a commitment to silence, true loyalty meant honoring each other's truths and supporting each other's paths to healing.

This new understanding was liberating. It allowed me to reframe my relationship with my family, moving away from the idea that loyalty required secrecy. Instead, I embraced the idea that loyalty could be built on honesty, compassion, and the courage to address difficult truths. By supporting one another's experiences, we were forming a new kind of family bond—one that valued openness over silence and resilience over avoidance. This was the kind of loyalty I wanted to cultivate, a loyalty that allowed each of us to grow beyond the limitations of our past.

However, this shift was not without its challenges. I quickly discovered that while some family members were willing to engage in this new approach, others remained rigidly attached to the old ways. They saw my openness as a threat to the family's reputation, a disruption to the image they had worked so hard to maintain. This resistance was difficult to face, especially when it came from those who had been closest to me. It reminded me that not everyone would be ready to embrace this new definition of loyalty, and that was something I had to accept.

Navigating these mixed reactions required a careful balance of courage and restraint. I had to remind myself that while I could not control others' responses, I could control my own. I chose to honor their feelings, even if I could not agree with their perspective. This approach allowed me to maintain a sense of peace, even when conversations became difficult. I found that by holding space for their views without letting go of my own, I could remain grounded in my journey without compromising my boundaries.

This experience taught me the value of holding two truths at once. I could be loyal to my family by respecting their perspectives, even as I remained loyal to my own path. This dual loyalty required constant mindfulness, an ability to navigate the spaces between acceptance and authenticity. It reminded me that family dynamics are often complex, shaped by layers of history and emotion that cannot be undone with a single conversation or change in perspective.

As I leaned into this new understanding of loyalty, I felt a growing sense of freedom. I was no longer bound by the need to fit into a predefined role or adhere to unspoken expectations. Instead, I allowed myself to fully embrace my journey, trusting that my path was valid, even if it diverged from the family's established narrative. This freedom was empowering, a reminder that I could honor my family while still honoring myself—a balance that allowed me to stay true to both my roots and my growth.

Reflections on Redefining Family Loyalty

1. **Embrace Loyalty as Support, Not Silence**: Redefine loyalty as a commitment to honoring each other's experiences. Support family members in their truths rather than adhering to outdated expectations of silence.

2. **Accept Mixed Reactions with Grace**: Understand that not everyone will share your perspective on family loyalty. Hold space for their views without compromising your own path.

3. **Balance Acceptance and Authenticity**: Recognize that loyalty to family and loyalty to self can coexist. Mindfully navigate these dynamics to stay true to both your roots and your journey forward.

As I moved further into this journey of redefining family loyalty, I realized that true loyalty required a commitment to growth, both personal and collective. It was not enough to simply maintain the status quo or uphold traditions that no longer served us. Real loyalty meant challenging each other to grow, to confront the truths that had long been hidden, and to create an environment where honesty could flourish. This understanding was empowering, yet it also came with a sense of responsibility that I had not anticipated.

With each family member who shared their story, I became more aware of the healing potential that lay within our connections. Every story offered a chance to bridge gaps, to mend wounds that had existed for generations. I felt a renewed commitment to this path, knowing that by embracing my truth, I was helping others find the courage to do the same. But I also knew that healing was not something I could force. Each of us had to come to it in our own time, and while I could offer support, I had to respect the pace at which others were willing—or able—to move.

This journey also taught me to be patient with myself. There were moments when I questioned whether I was strong enough to hold both my healing and the complex emotions of those around me. I sometimes wondered if it would be easier to retreat, to return to a life of silence rather than facing the tension that truth often brings. But in these moments of doubt, I reminded myself of the strength it had taken to reach this point, the resilience I had cultivated through years of confronting painful truths. I had already walked through fire; I could continue to hold this space, even when it felt heavy.

Reflecting on this, I found a renewed sense of purpose in my journey. My story, while deeply personal, was no longer just mine alone. It was part of a larger tapestry, a collective journey of healing that held the potential to change the dynamics within our family. This shared healing was more than I had ever expected when I first began to speak my truth. It was a reminder that healing is a ripple effect, touching lives in ways we may never fully see or understand.

Through this process, I learned to honor both the shared and individual aspects of our journeys. While our paths intersected, each of us had our own work to do, our own truths to confront, and our own healing to embrace. This understanding allowed me to find peace in the complexity of family dynamics, to hold space for others without compromising my own growth. It was a delicate balance, a constant practice of compassion, resilience, and respect.

In closing this chapter of new revelations, I felt a profound sense of gratitude for the strength that had carried me through. I had found my own voice, my own courage, and in doing so, I had helped to create a space where others could find theirs. This journey was far from over, but I knew that whatever lay ahead, I would face it with the same resilience that had brought me this far. I was no longer alone in my healing; I was part of a family that, despite its imperfections, was learning to grow together, one story at a time.

Key Takeaways on Embracing Growth Through Family Connections

1. **Cultivate a Commitment to Growth**: Embrace loyalty that supports growth rather than maintaining the status quo. True loyalty invites

us to challenge each other toward healing and authenticity.

2. **Respect Individual Paces in Healing**: Understand that each person's journey is unique. Offer support without trying to control or accelerate others' healing processes.

3. **Find Strength in Shared and Individual Journeys**: Honor the collective journey of healing while recognizing that each family member has their own path. This balance allows for personal growth within the shared family narrative.

CHAPTER 4

Navigating Boundaries: Protecting Peace and Self-Worth

Reflecting on the journey that brought me to this point, I realized that resilience was at the core of everything I had faced and overcome. Every challenge, every moment of doubt or heartbreak, had deepened my strength. Yet, resilience was not a trait I had always recognized in myself. It was something I discovered slowly, one experience at a time, like collecting pieces of armor to protect my heart and spirit. With each trial, I built a foundation of resilience, a well of strength that sustained me when the weight of truth and family history felt too heavy to bear.

Resilience, I found, was not about enduring hardship without feeling pain. It was about allowing myself to feel deeply, to grieve, to struggle, and then, slowly, to rise again. Early on, I had believed that resilience meant pushing through challenges without acknowledging the pain they caused. But as I grew, I learned that true resilience was about acceptance—about letting each experience transform me, even when that transformation was difficult or painful. It was the ability to look at my own reflection, acknowledge the scars, and understand that they were part of my strength.

One of the most important practices I embraced to nurture resilience was self-reflection. Taking time to look inward, to explore my feelings, and to understand my reactions allowed me to ground myself, especially during challenging times. Self-reflection helped me see patterns in my thoughts and emotions, guiding me toward a deeper understanding of who I was becoming through this journey. By examining my fears, my hopes, and my pain, I was able to find clarity and purpose, even when circumstances were complex and difficult.

Mindfulness became another essential part of my resilience toolkit. Through mindfulness, I learned to stay present in each moment, to embrace my experiences without judgment, and to release the need to control every outcome. Practicing mindfulness helped me create a space within myself where I could find calm amid the storms of life.

49

This inner sanctuary allowed me to respond to challenges with greater patience and compassion, both for myself and for others. In moments of difficulty, mindfulness reminded me that I was more than my circumstances—I was a whole, evolving person with the power to navigate any challenge.

Setting boundaries is not about shutting others out but about protecting the space you need to heal. When I faced resistance from family, I felt torn between wanting to connect and needing to preserve my peace. Boundaries became my sanctuary, a way to engage with compassion while maintaining self-respect. During these moments, I allowed myself to step back, to breathe, and to nurture my own needs. I came to understand that resilience was not about constant action; it was about finding balance, about knowing when to push forward and when to rest. This balance, I realized, was what allowed me to continue my journey sustainably, without burning out or losing my sense of self.

As I reflected on these practices, I saw how each one had contributed to my sense of inner strength. Resilience, I learned, was something I could cultivate daily, even in small ways. It was a journey, a gradual process of building a foundation that would carry me through both the light and dark moments of life. With each step forward, I grew more connected to myself, more confident in my ability to face the unknown with courage and grace. This resilience was not only a source of strength; it was a gift I could offer to myself, a reminder that I had the power to heal and grow, no matter what lay ahead.

Practical Practices for Cultivating Resilience

1. **Embrace Self-Reflection**: Dedicate time to examine your feelings, reactions, and inner landscape. Self-reflection fosters clarity and deepens your connection to yourself.
2. **Practice Mindfulness Daily**: Use mindfulness techniques to stay present and grounded. This practice creates an inner calm that supports resilience during difficult times.
3. **Allow Space for Rest and Renewal**: Recognize when you need to step back. Resting is not a weakness; it is a vital part of sustaining resilience and preserving your energy.

In my journey toward resilience, I learned that self-compassion was a crucial component. It became clear to me that resilience was not just about overcoming obstacles—it was about embracing my humanity, understanding that I could be both strong and vulnerable at the same time. Self-compassion allowed me to forgive myself for moments of doubt, for times when I needed to pause, or when I felt uncertain about my path. In these moments, self-compassion reminded me that I was worthy of kindness, even when I struggled.

One of the most profound ways I practiced self-compassion was through acknowledging my feelings without judgment. Whenever I felt fear, sadness, or frustration, I allowed myself to fully experience those emotions rather than suppressing them. This approach was a significant shift from how I used to handle emotions. In the past, I would try to "stay strong" by pushing feelings aside, believing that resilience meant ignoring pain. But I realized that true strength lay in honoring those emotions, in giving myself the space to feel without criticism or shame.

Practicing self-compassion also required me to let go of perfectionism. I had often believed that I needed to be flawless in my healing journey—that any setback was a sign of weakness or failure. This belief weighed heavily on me, creating an internal pressure that was as exhausting as it was unrealistic. Letting go of perfectionism was liberating; it allowed me to see my journey as one of growth, where missteps were simply part of the process. By releasing the need for perfection, I made room for grace, learning to see myself with a gentler, more forgiving perspective.

In cultivating this perspective, I began to understand that resilience was not a fixed destination. It was a continuous practice, something that needed to be nurtured daily. Just as a garden needs sunlight, water, and care, my resilience required attention, patience, and the willingness to show up for myself, no matter what. Some days, resilience meant finding joy in small moments or appreciating the progress

I had made. Other days, it meant simply getting through, surviving another day with the intention to try again tomorrow.

As I continued to grow in resilience, I realized that I could offer this same compassion to others. The more I nurtured kindness within myself, the more I found myself naturally extending it to those around me. I was able to empathize with family members who were on their own journeys, who were navigating their own struggles and challenges. By embracing my humanity, I was able to see humanity in others, recognizing that we were all doing our best with the resources we had. This realization created a sense of connection, a reminder that resilience could be a bridge that brought us closer together.

Reflecting on these practices, I felt a renewed sense of strength. Resilience was no longer an ideal I was striving to reach; it was a way of living, a foundation that supported me through every experience, whether joyful or painful. This resilience was rooted in kindness, patience, and the understanding that my journey, with all its difficulties, was valuable. I came to see that resilience was not about becoming unbreakable; it was about learning to bend without losing myself, to face life's challenges with an open heart and a compassionate spirit.

Guidelines for Embracing Resilience Through Self-Compassion

1. **Honor Your Feelings Without Judgment**: Allow yourself to experience emotions fully. Embracing vulnerability strengthens resilience.
2. **Release Perfectionism in Your Healing**: Let go of the need to be flawless. View each step, even setbacks, as part of the growth process.
3. **Practice Daily Acts of Self-Kindness**: Nurture resilience with small, consistent acts of compassion. Recognize that resilience is a journey, one that requires patience and gentleness.

In building resilience, I discovered that one of the most valuable tools was learning to reframe my challenges. Life was not always going to go according to plan, and setbacks were inevitable. In the past, I would view these obstacles as failures or signs that I was not progressing quickly enough. But as I continued this journey, I began to see challenges as opportunities—moments that allowed me to grow, to deepen my understanding of myself, and to strengthen my ability to adapt. This shift in perspective was transformative; it allowed me to approach life's uncertainties with a sense of curiosity rather than fear.

Reframing challenges was not about denying the difficulty or pain of those moments. Instead, it was about choosing to see them as part of a larger narrative, one where each experience contributed to my growth. This practice gave me the strength to face discomfort with an open mind. Whenever a setback occurred, I asked myself, "What is this here to teach me?" Sometimes the answer came easily, revealing a lesson about patience or resilience. Other times, the lesson was subtle, something that only became clear as I reflected on its weeks or months later. But by viewing challenges as teachers, I found a sense of purpose in each experience, even when it was difficult.

An essential part of resilience was also learning to cultivate hope, especially during times when hope felt elusive. There were moments on this journey when the weight of the past felt overwhelming, when I wondered if healing was even possible. In those moments, I turned to small practices that helped me rekindle hope. I reminded myself of the progress I had already made, the strength I had shown, and the resilience that had carried me through previous hardships. I surrounded myself with reminders of joy and gratitude, whether through a meaningful conversation with a friend, a quiet walk in nature, or time spent reflecting on memories of kindness and connection.

In nurturing hope, I found that even the smallest acts of self-care could make a profound difference. Sometimes, simply allowing myself a few moments of quiet reflection or gratitude shifted my perspective, giving me the strength to face another day with courage. I realized that hope was not about believing that everything would always be easy or that I would be free from pain. Rather, hope was about trusting that I could face whatever came my way, that I had the tools and resilience to navigate even the most challenging moments.

As I continued to practice resilience, I also learned the importance of celebrating progress, no matter how small. Healing is not a linear journey; it is a path filled with peaks and valleys, with moments of breakthrough and moments of doubt. By acknowledging each step forward, I was able to cultivate a sense of accomplishment and pride in my journey. These celebrations did not have to be grand gestures; sometimes, simply recognizing a moment of courage or a day of peace was enough to reinforce my strength.

Resilience, I learned, was a mosaic—a collection of practices, perspectives, and small acts of self-compassion that came together to form a foundation of inner strength. Each lesson, each moment of growth, contributed to a larger picture, one that reminded me of my capacity to heal, to grow, and to thrive. This resilience was not just a survival mechanism; it was a testament to my journey, a symbol of the courage and grace that had carried me through. It was a gift I could carry, a reminder that I could face life's challenges with an open heart and a steadfast spirit.

Practical Steps for Strengthening
Resilience Through Reframing and Hope

1. **Reframe Challenges as Opportunities**: When facing setbacks, ask yourself what the experience can teach you. Reframing obstacles as growth opportunities strengthens resilience.

2. **Cultivate Small Acts of Hope**: Engage in daily practices that nurture hope, whether through gratitude, connection, or moments of self-reflection. Hope sustains resilience in difficult times.

3. **Celebrate Every Step Forward**: Recognize and honor each moment of progress. Celebrating small victories reinforces strength and builds confidence in your journey.

As I deepened my understanding of resilience, I began to recognize the importance of adaptability. Life, I had come to understand, is unpredictable. No matter how carefully we plan or how much we try to control outcomes, there are always events beyond our influence. Resilience, therefore, was as much about adapting to change as it was about standing firm in the face of hardship. Embracing adaptability allowed me to flow with life's uncertainties, to find stability not by rigidly holding onto my expectations but by learning to shift when necessary.

Adaptability also taught me to appreciate the wisdom that comes from change. Each unexpected turn in my journey brought new insights, often revealing strengths I did not know I had. For instance, when I faced moments of doubt or confusion, I learned to view them as invitations to explore different paths, to consider perspectives I might have overlooked. This flexibility became a form of resilience, reminding me that there are many ways to navigate life's challenges and that sometimes, taking an unexpected route, led to the most profound growth.

Practicing adaptability required me to stay open to the unknown, to approach each new situation with a sense of curiosity rather than resistance. I realized that resilience was not just about overcoming what was difficult—it was about welcoming the unfamiliar with an open heart, trusting that I had the inner resources to handle whatever came my way. This openness brought a sense of freedom; it allowed me to experience life with less fear and more acceptance, knowing that I could adapt to any circumstances without losing myself in the process.

Alongside adaptability, I also found the importance of setting intentions in my journey. While I could not control every outcome, I could shape my journey by being intentional in my choices. Setting intentions became a way of directing my energy, of grounding myself in the values and goals that mattered most to me. Whether it was an intention to approach challenges with patience, to practice kindness in difficult moments, or to trust in my own resilience, these intentions helped anchor me in times of uncertainty.

Intentions offered a sense of purpose, a reminder that while I could not predict the future, I could still choose how I moved through it. By setting intentions, I created a path that aligned with my values, allowing me to face each day with a sense of clarity and direction. This practice gave me a feeling of empowerment, a reminder that I had agency over my journey, even when the circumstances around me were beyond my control.

Reflecting on these lessons, I saw that resilience was a dynamic quality—one that required both flexibility and focus, adaptability, and intention. It was not a one-size-fits-all solution to life's challenges but a mosaic of practices that allowed me to navigate each experience with grace. Resilience, I learned, was about finding harmony within myself, about balancing the need for strength with the wisdom of flexibility. It was about embracing life fully, trusting in my own capacity to grow and adapt, and moving forward with courage and intention.

Key Insights for Building Resilience Through Adaptability and Intention

1. **Embrace Adaptability as a Strength**: Allow yourself to shift and grow with life's changes. Adaptability fosters resilience by enabling you to face uncertainty with confidence.

2. **Set Intentions to Guide Your Path**: Ground yourself in your values and goals through intentional choices. Setting intentions helps create a sense of purpose, even in unpredictable times.

3. **Find Balance Between Flexibility and Focus**: Cultivate a resilience that blends adaptability with a clear sense of direction. This balance allows you to move forward with both grace and intention.

As I continued practicing resilience through adaptability and intention, I discovered a deeper layer of inner strength. I began to recognize that resilience was not only about facing challenges but also about maintaining faith in my journey, even during times of uncertainty. This faith was not tied to a specific outcome; instead, it was a quiet trust in my own capacity to handle whatever came my way. It was the confidence that, regardless of external circumstances, I could find my way forward with integrity and grace.

Developing this inner faith required me to let go of the need for certainty. I had always been someone who found comfort in knowing the next step, in having a clear plan and direction. But resilience taught me that life rarely unfolds in predictable ways. Instead, I learned to embrace uncertainty as a natural part of growth. By surrendering the need to know every detail of the journey, I opened myself to possibilities that I might have missed if I had been too focused on a single outcome.

In embracing uncertainty, I found myself leaning more deeply into trust—not only trust in myself but in the process of life itself. Trust became a cornerstone of my resilience, a foundation that supported me even when the path was unclear. This trust was not blind faith; it was a grounded belief that I could meet each moment with authenticity, that I had the inner resources to adapt and grow, no matter what challenges arose. Trust allowed me to move forward without fear, to view each experience as an opportunity for discovery rather than a threat to my stability.

Building resilience also taught me the value of gratitude. During challenges, gratitude became a way to reconnect with moments of joy and abundance, even when life felt difficult. By focusing on what I appreciated, I shifted my perspective, finding strength in the blessings I already had. Whether it was a meaningful conversation, a moment of peace, or a small achievement, gratitude allowed me to ground myself in positivity, to see the beauty and resilience that existed alongside my struggles.

Reflecting on gratitude reminded me that resilience was as much about appreciating the journey as it was about overcoming hardships. I began to see each challenge as part of a larger tapestry, one that included both joy and sorrow, growth, and rest. Gratitude became a practice of honoring the fullness of life, of recognizing that resilience was not just about surviving difficult moments—it was about embracing the richness of each experience, finding value in both the light and the shadows.

As I closed this chapter on resilience, I felt a profound sense of peace. Resilience was no longer just a concept; it was a way of being, a presence within me that I could rely on at every step of my journey. This resilience was rooted in adaptability, in intentional living, in trust, and in gratitude. It was a mosaic of practices and perspectives that transformed how I faced challenges and experienced life. With resilience as my guide, I felt ready to embrace whatever lay ahead, confident in my ability to navigate the unknown with strength and grace.

Reflections on Resilience Through Trust and Gratitude

1. **Embrace Uncertainty as Part of Growth**: Release the need for certainty and view the unknown as a space for discovery. Trust in your capacity to handle whatever comes.

2. **Cultivate Trust in Yourself and the Journey**: Ground yourself in the belief that you can meet each moment authentically. This trust creates a foundation of resilience that supports you through change.

3. **Practice Gratitude to Anchor Positivity**: Focus on moments of joy and appreciation, even in challenging times. Gratitude enriches resilience, allowing you to find beauty in every part of the journey.

CHAPTER 5

Anchoring Self-Worth: Rediscovering Identity and Strength

As I reflected on my journey, I came to understand that forgiveness was not just an act; it was a way of life, a path to freedom that required courage, compassion, and a willingness to let go of what no longer served me. Forgiveness, I realized, was not about condoning harm or erasing painful memories. Instead, it was about releasing the hold that resentment and anger had on my heart. It was a choice to free me from the weight of past hurts, to create space for peace and healing within.

At first, the idea of forgiveness felt daunting. I had spent years carrying the pain of past experiences, allowing them to shape how I saw myself and others. There was a part of me that feared letting go of this hurt, as if releasing it would somehow invalidate my experiences. But as I delved deeper into my healing, I began to see that holding onto anger only kept me tethered to the past, limiting my ability to fully embrace the present. Forgiveness, I learned, was a gift I could offer myself—a way to unburden my soul and make room for joy and growth.

Forgiving others required me to look at their actions with compassion, to see them not only through the lens of my own pain but through a broader perspective. I began to understand that, like me, others were shaped by their own histories, fears, and limitations. This did not excuse their actions or negate the impact of their choices, but it did allow me to recognize that they, too, were navigating their own struggles. Seeing them in this light softened my heart, allowing me to let go of the bitterness that had once consumed me.

An essential part of this process was forgiving myself. For so long, I had been hard on myself for choices I made in the past, for moments of weakness, for not healing "fast enough." I realized that I had been carrying shame and guilt, believing that I should have somehow done things differently. Self-forgiveness required me to release these expectations, to understand that I had done the best I could with the resources and knowledge I had at the time. In forgiving myself, I found a new sense of compassion, a gentle acceptance of my own humanity.

This journey taught me that forgiveness is not a single act but a continuous practice. There were days when I felt at peace, and others when old wounds resurfaced, bringing back memories I thought I had moved beyond. On those days, I reminded myself that healing was not linear—that forgiveness was a commitment to releasing anger and hurt, even if it had to be done repeatedly. This understanding allowed me to approach forgiveness with patience, accepting that some days would be harder than others, and that was okay.

As I continued to practice forgiveness, I felt a profound sense of liberation. Forgiveness was not about forgetting or excusing harm; it was about reclaiming my own power, choosing to let go of what no longer served me. This freedom allowed me to move forward without the weight of the past holding me back. Forgiveness became a path to peace, a way of saying to myself, "I deserve to live unburdened, to experience joy and love without the shadow of resentment." In embracing forgiveness, I found a renewed sense of hope and the courage to create a future rooted in compassion and kindness.

Practical Steps for Embracing Forgiveness

1. **See Others with Compassion:** Acknowledge that others are shaped by their own experiences. Forgiving does not excuse their actions but allows you to release resentment.

2. **Practice Self-Forgiveness:** Let go of guilt and self-judgment. Embrace your past choices with compassion, knowing you did the best you could at the time.

3. **Approach Forgiveness as an Ongoing Practice:** Accept that forgiveness is not a one-time act. Allow yourself patience and kindness as you continue to release anger and hurt over time.

As I continued the path of forgiveness, I discovered that letting go required a conscious decision each day. Forgiveness was not a one-time event; it was a practice of release, a commitment to freeing myself from the past. I began to understand that forgiving someone did not mean I would never feel pain again or that the memories would vanish. Instead, forgiveness was about choosing not to let those memories control my life. It was about reclaiming my own narrative, taking back the power to define my experiences without being overshadowed by hurt.

This practice of letting go was not always easy. There were days when old memories resurfaced when resentment would quietly seep back into my thoughts. In those moments, I reminded myself of the reasons I chose forgiveness in the first place: for my peace, for my growth, and for the freedom to live unburdened by the past. I began to see forgiveness as an act of courage, a way of honoring my journey by releasing the emotions that no longer served me. Each time I let go, I felt a little lighter, a little more connected to the life I was creating for myself.

One of the most powerful realizations I had was that forgiveness did not mean reconciling with everyone who had caused me pain. Forgiveness, I learned, was something I could do for myself, regardless of the actions or intentions of others. There were people I chose to forgive without reestablishing a relationship, understanding that forgiveness was a gift I gave myself. This boundary allowed me to protect my well-being while still practicing compassion. It reminded me that I could honor my own healing without needing validation or apology from others.

This understanding of boundaries within forgiveness transformed how I viewed my relationships. I learned that it was possible to forgive someone while still setting limits that protected my peace. Forgiveness did not require me to invite people back into my life if their presence disrupted my well-being. Instead, it allowed me to let go of resentment while honoring the boundaries I needed to thrive. This balance gave me a sense of empowerment, a reminder that forgiveness and boundaries could coexist harmoniously.

In practicing forgiveness, I also came to realize the importance of forgiveness as an act of self-respect. By choosing to forgive, I was affirming my own worth, acknowledging that I deserved a life free from the weight of past hurts. I began to see forgiveness as a way of honoring my own heart, of recognizing that I was worthy of peace and joy. This self-respect fueled my commitment to the path of forgiveness, reminding me that letting go was an act of love, both for myself and for the life I was building.

Through this journey, I found a sense of liberation I had not expected. Forgiveness had once seemed like a sacrifice; a concession I was not sure I was willing to make. But as I embraced it more fully, I realized that forgiveness was not a loss; it was a profound gain. It was the freedom to live on my own terms, to create a future unbound by past hurts. This path of forgiveness became a path of self-discovery, one that allowed me to step into my life with a renewed sense of purpose and clarity.

Boundaries and Self-Respect in Forgiveness

1. **Forgive Without Reconciliation if Needed**: Understand that forgiveness does not require reconciling with those who caused harm. Forgive for your peace, even if boundaries remain.
2. **Set Boundaries to Protect Your Peace**: Establish limits that support your well-being. Forgiveness

and boundaries can coexist, allowing you to maintain both compassion and self-care.

3. **Embrace Forgiveness as Self-Respect:** Recognize that letting go honors your own worth. Forgiveness is an act of love for yourself, affirming that you deserve a life unburdened by past hurt.

As I continued on this journey, I came to understand that forgiveness was not a linear path. There were times when old wounds resurfaced, when moments of anger or hurt would revisit my heart. In those times, I realized that forgiveness was like a muscle that needed to be strengthened over time. Each moment of letting go was an act of resilience, a commitment to peace, and a step forward on my path to freedom. It was in these recurring challenges that I found the depth of forgiveness—not as a one-time release, but as a continuous process of choosing freedom over pain.

One of the most helpful practices I embraced was mindfulness. By staying present, I was able to witness my emotions without judgment, to observe anger, sadness, or frustration as they arose without allowing them to consume me. Mindfulness allowed me to see these emotions as passing experiences rather than fixed states. Instead of reacting to them, I could choose to breathe, to acknowledge my feelings, and then to gently release them. This practice became an anchor, a way to maintain my balance and peace even when difficult memories resurfaced.

Another valuable lesson I learned was the power of reframing my perspective. Rather than viewing forgiveness as something I "owed" to others, I began to see it as an opportunity to free myself. By reframing forgiveness as an act of self-liberation, I shifted my focus from what others deserved to what I deserved—a life that was not weighed down by resentment or pain. This new perspective was empowering; it allowed me to reclaim my energy, to channel my focus toward my growth and healing rather than lingering on past hurts.

Through reframing, I also found a way to transform my experiences into wisdom. Each hurtful event, each painful memory, had taught me something valuable—about myself, about resilience, and about the kind of life I wanted to create. By seeing my experiences as lessons rather than burdens, I was able to find meaning in them, to understand that they had shaped me in ways that served my growth. This perspective gave me a sense of purpose; it reminded me that even the most challenging experiences could be catalysts for healing and transformation.

As I practiced forgiveness, I noticed that my relationships with others began to change as well. With a heart less burdened by resentment, I found myself more open to connection, more willing to approach others with empathy and understanding. Forgiveness had softened my edges, allowing me to see the humanity in others, to recognize that they, too, were on their own journeys of growth and healing. This shift did not mean I ignored past hurts or dismissed boundaries—it simply meant that I could approach relationships from a place of compassion rather than defensiveness.

In reclaiming my story, I rediscovered my sense of self-worth. For years, I measured my value through the lens of others—seeking approval, avoiding conflict, and suppressing my truth. But as I shared my journey, I realized my worth was not tied to external validation but to the strength I had cultivated within.

Self-worth is not about perfection. It is about accepting yourself as you are, scars and all, and finding value in every stage of the journey. By letting go of perfectionism, I found freedom in being my authentic self, unbound by the need for approval or understanding from others. Reflecting on these changes, I felt a profound sense of gratitude for the journey of forgiveness. It had not been easy, nor was it complete, but it had brought me to a place of inner peace I had not known before. Forgiveness was not about absolution or forgetting; it was about honoring my own path, my own growth, and my own worth.

Practices for Deepening Forgiveness and Reclaiming Peace

1. **Embrace Mindfulness to Observe Emotions**: Practice staying present with your emotions without judgment. Mindfulness allows you to witness anger or hurt temporarily, creating space for release.

2. **Reframe Forgiveness as Self-Liberation**: See forgiveness as an act of freedom rather than something owed. This perspective empowers you to focus on your own healing and well-being.

3. **Find Wisdom in Past Experiences**: Transform your challenges into lessons that serve your growth. Recognize that even painful memories can become sources of resilience and understanding.

In this journey, forgiveness was closely tied to acceptance. Forgiveness did not require me to erase the past or pretend it had not shaped me. Instead, it required me to accept what had happened, to acknowledge the impact of those experiences, and to let go of the need to rewrite history. Acceptance became a form of freedom—a way to make peace with the past without allowing it to dictate my present or future.

Learning to accept was challenging, especially when I thought of the pain and losses, I had experienced. But over time, I realized that acceptance was not a sign of weakness or surrender. It was an act of strength, a choice to acknowledge reality without resistance. Acceptance allowed me to release the "what-ifs" and "if-onlys" that had haunted me. By embracing acceptance, I could say, "This happened, and it hurt—but it doesn't define who I am." This perspective gave me the clarity to see beyond the pain and to envision a life that was shaped but not controlled by the past.

An important part of acceptance was recognizing that some things may never be fully understood. There were questions that would go unanswered, motivations that would remain unclear, and actions that would continue to feel senseless. Acceptance meant letting go of the need for perfect closure. Instead of seeking definitive answers, I found peace in accepting the ambiguity, in trusting that I could move forward even without understanding everything. This release of control brought a sense of calm; it reminded me that I did not need every piece of the puzzle to feel whole.

Acceptance also extended to me. I learned to accept the person I had become because of my experiences—the strength, the scars, and the resilience that had formed over time. By accepting myself as I was, I stopped trying to meet an idealized version of healing or wholeness. Instead, I embraced my journey with all its imperfections. This self-acceptance allowed me to approach each day with compassion, to understand that healing was a continuous process and that I was worthy of love and respect at every stage of that journey.

Reflecting on acceptance, I realized that forgiveness, at its core, was a way of reclaiming my peace. By forgiving others and myself, I was choosing to live in the present rather than being trapped in the past. Forgiveness became a foundation for a life rooted in freedom, compassion, and resilience. It reminded me that while I could not change what had happened, I had the power to shape how I responded to it. This realization was liberating; it allowed me to reclaim my story, to live as the author of my own life, unbound by the weight of past pains.

With forgiveness and acceptance as my companions, I found a sense of wholeness. I was no longer seeking something external to complete me; instead, I felt a quiet, inner completeness that came from honoring my journey. Forgiveness had taught me the strength of letting go, and acceptance had shown me the peace of embracing what was. Together, they became the pillars that supported my growth, guiding me toward a life of freedom and inner harmony.

Guidelines for Embracing Forgiveness and Acceptance

1. **Release the Need for Closure**: Understand that some things may never be fully understood. Embrace ambiguity and trust that you can move forward without perfect answers.

2. **Accept Yourself as You Are**: Embrace your journey with compassion, understanding that healing is imperfect. Self-acceptance allows you to approach each day with grace and resilience.

3. **Reclaim Your Peace Through Forgiveness**: Choose to live in the present, unburdened by the past. Forgiveness and acceptance become a foundation for inner freedom and wholeness.

As I neared the end of this journey into forgiveness, I found myself reflecting on the ways it had transformed not only my heart but also my outlook on life. Forgiveness had been a profound teacher, revealing to me the strength that comes from letting go and the peace that emerges when I release the need for control. It had shown me that true freedom comes not from holding on but from releasing, from trusting that I could face the world unburdened by past hurts. This newfound freedom was not about forgetting what had happened; it was about choosing to move forward with love, courage, and an open heart.

One of the most powerful lessons I learned through forgiveness was the importance of cultivating gratitude. As I released the weight of resentment, I found myself more attuned to the blessings in my life—the moments of kindness, the friendships that lifted me, and the simple joys that enriched my days. Gratitude became a way to anchor myself in the present, to focus on what brought me peace and happiness rather than what had caused me pain. By practicing gratitude, I was able to create a space for love, for joy, and for a future filled with possibility.

Gratitude also allowed me to reframe my past experiences. Instead of seeing them solely as sources of pain, I began to recognize the resilience they had helped me build, the wisdom they had imparted, and the compassion they had nurtured within me. I could honor these experiences without being defined by them, finding a balance that allowed me to move forward with strength. This perspective shift gave me the courage to continue my path, trusting that every experience, even the difficult ones, had a role in shaping the person I was becoming.

As I looked to the future, I felt a renewed sense of hope and purpose. Forgiveness had cleared a path for me to live with intention, to approach each day as an opportunity to gain experience, to love, and to create a life aligned with my deepest values. I realized that the journey of forgiveness was not only about healing the past; it was about embracing the future with a heart free from the chains of resentment.

This freedom allowed me to dream, to set new goals, and to step into the next chapter of my life with confidence.

Reflecting on this journey, I felt immense gratitude for the strength and resilience that had carried me through. Forgiveness has taught me the power of release, the importance of self-compassion, and the beauty of acceptance. It had allowed me to reclaim my peace, to rewrite my story with love and integrity, and to create a foundation of inner harmony that would support me through all of life's challenges. With forgiveness as my guide, I knew that I could face the future with an open heart, ready to embrace whatever came my way.

In closing, I understood that forgiveness was not an endpoint but a way of life—a continuous choice to live with compassion, to release what no longer served me, and to create a life rooted in peace and wholeness. This journey had transformed me in ways I had not anticipated, deepening my capacity for love, my commitment to growth, and my understanding of what it meant to live freely. Forgiveness was a gift I would carry forward, a reminder that true strength lies not in holding on but in letting go.

Reflections on a Life of Forgiveness and Freedom

1. **Embrace Gratitude as a Foundation for Peace**: Focus on the blessings in your life. Gratitude helps to shift your perspective toward the positive, creating space for love and joy.

2. **Reframe the Past with Compassion**: Honor your experiences as sources of strength and resilience. See them as parts of your journey that contributed to your growth.

3. **Choose Forgiveness as a Way of Life**: Let forgiveness be a guiding principle, a continuous choice to live unburdened by resentment. This practice cultivates inner freedom and harmony.

CHAPTER 6

Navigating Family Healing: Rebuilding Trust and Connection

As I continued on my journey toward healing, I came to understand that setting boundaries was essential for protecting my well-being and nurturing my growth. Boundaries were not about building walls to keep people out; rather, they were about creating a safe space within myself, a space where I could thrive without compromising my values, needs, or peace. For so long, I had believed that setting boundaries might make me appear distant or unkind, but I realized that true compassion begins with self-respect. By honoring my own limits, I could be present in my relationships with authenticity and integrity.

Setting boundaries required me to identify my personal limits—the emotional, physical, and mental thresholds that defined what I was willing to accept. These limits were not rigid; they evolved with time, reflecting the changes in my needs and values. Recognizing these boundaries was a process of self-awareness, one that required me to listen closely to my inner voice, to understand when something felt out of alignment. Each time I honored a boundary, I strengthened my connection to myself, reinforcing a foundation of self-trust and respect.

Communicating these boundaries to others was a challenging but necessary step. I had often avoided asserting my needs out of fear of conflict or rejection, but I realized that silence only led to resentment and exhaustion. By expressing my boundaries with kindness and clarity, I could share my needs without placing blame or guilt on others. I learned to say, "This is what I need to feel safe," or "This is how I can be my best self," and to trust that those who valued me would understand. Boundaries became a way to build healthier connections, allowing me to show up in relationships with a sense of peace rather than obligation.

One of the most important lessons I learned was that boundaries are not static; they require ongoing reflection and adjustment. Just as we grow and change, so do our needs. There were times when I realized that a boundary I had set needed to be revisited, that I needed to expand or shift it to reflect where I was in my journey. This flexibility allowed me to maintain a sense of balance, to honor my growth without feeling confined by past decisions. By remaining open to change, I could adapt my boundaries to support my evolving self, ensuring that they served my well-being rather than limiting my experiences.

As I embraced the practice of setting boundaries, I noticed a profound shift in my inner peace. Boundaries became a way to protect my energy, to preserve my emotional and mental health, and to create a life that felt true to who I was. They allowed me to engage in relationships with honesty, to give from a place of abundance rather than depletion. Setting boundaries was not only an act of self-care; it was an act of self-love, a way of affirming that my needs and feelings mattered.

Reflecting on this journey, I saw that boundaries were not barriers; they were pathways to deeper connection and understanding. By respecting my own limits, I could approach life with clarity and confidence, knowing that I had the tools to protect my peace while still being open to others. Boundaries had given me a newfound sense of freedom—a freedom to be myself, to honor my values, and to create relationships rooted in mutual respect and compassion.

Practical Steps for Setting Healthy Boundaries

1. **Identify Your Personal Limits**: Reflect on your emotional, physical, and mental needs. Recognizing these limits helps you define boundaries that protect your well-being.

2. **Communicate Boundaries with Kindness**: Express your needs clearly and compassionately. Communicating boundaries builds understanding and strengthens relationships.

3. **Revisit and Adjust Boundaries as Needed**: Allow boundaries to evolve with your growth. Flexibility ensures that your boundaries support, rather than confine, your journey.

As I grew more comfortable setting boundaries, I began to understand that boundaries were not only beneficial for me but also for those around me. In the past, I had often tried to accommodate everyone's needs, sometimes at the expense of my own well-being. But over time, I realized that by setting clear boundaries, I was giving others the gift of knowing where I stood. Boundaries created a sense of clarity and respect, allowing people to engage with me in a way that honored both their needs and mine. This mutual respect was the foundation for healthier, more fulfilling relationships.

One of the most valuable lessons I learned was that boundaries are expressions of my values. Each boundary I set reflected something important to me—a commitment to self-care, a dedication to personal growth, or a respect for my time and energy. When I viewed boundaries through this lens, I no longer saw them as acts of rejection or isolation. Instead, I saw them as acts of alignment, ways to live in harmony with my beliefs and priorities. This perspective allowed me to approach boundaries with a sense of purpose, knowing that each one contributed to a life that felt authentic and meaningful.

Setting boundaries also helped me cultivate resilience in the face of challenges. There were times when others did not understand or appreciate my boundaries, times when I faced resistance or criticism for asserting my needs. But each time I held firm, I strengthened my sense of self, reinforcing the knowledge that my well-being was worth protecting. I learned that I did not have to justify my boundaries to everyone, that they were valid simply because they reflected my needs. This resilience allowed me to stand confidently in my choices, even when they were not met with approval.

As I practiced setting boundaries, I also discovered the importance of flexibility. Boundaries were not meant to be rigid or unchanging; they were tools for navigating relationships and experiences. There were moments when I needed to adjust a boundary, to consider the unique circumstances of a situation or relationship. This flexibility did not weaken my boundaries; it allowed them to serve me more effectively, adapting to the flow of life while still protecting my core values. By balancing firmness with openness, I was able to create boundaries that felt both supportive and adaptable.

In reflecting on the impact of boundaries, I found a deeper appreciation for the peace they brought into my life. Boundaries allowed me to engage with others from a place of fullness rather than exhaustion, to give freely because I was not giving more than I could sustain. They created a sense of safety within myself, a foundation that supported my growth and well-being. With boundaries in place, I could approach relationships with empathy and presence, knowing that my needs were honored and protected.

Boundaries were a gift I gave to myself—a way to live with integrity, to nurture my well-being, and to build connections rooted in mutual respect. They reminded me that I had the power to shape my experiences, to create a life that felt aligned with my values and aspirations. Boundaries became a testament to my growth, a reminder of the strength it took to honor myself fully and to cultivate a life of peace and authenticity.

Reflections on Boundaries as Acts of Integrity and Peace

1. **Recognize Boundaries as Expressions of Values**: See boundaries as reflections of what matters most to you. Each boundary aligns you with your core beliefs and priorities.

2. **Build Resilience Through Boundaries**: Embrace the strength that comes from honoring your needs. Boundaries reinforce your sense of self and protect your well-being.

3. **Balance Flexibility and Firmness**: Allow boundaries to adapt to life's changes without compromising your values. Flexibility ensures that boundaries serve you effectively over time.

As I continued to explore the role of boundaries in my life, I realized that boundaries were also a way to practice empathy, both for myself and for others. When I honored my own limits, I was better able to understand and respect the boundaries of others. In the past, I had sometimes pushed against others' boundaries, not out of malice but because I did not fully understand the importance of honoring limits. Now, with my own experiences in mind, I can see boundaries as expressions of care and respect. This shift allowed me to approach relationships with a deeper sense of empathy, knowing that boundaries were not meant to create distance but to foster healthy connection.

Boundaries also required me to let go of the need to please everyone. I had often felt pressure to meet others' expectations, to say yes even when it meant stretching myself too thin. But as I grew more comfortable with boundaries, I learned that I did not need to please everyone to be worthy of connection. By choosing my well-being over the need for approval, I found a sense of freedom and self-worth that was not dependent on others' opinions. This change was liberating; it reminded me that my value was intrinsic, not something to be earned through endless acts of accommodation.

In practicing boundaries, I discovered the importance of consistency. Setting a boundary was only the first step; maintaining it required commitment and self-discipline. There were times when it was tempting to let a boundary slide, to compromise my needs for the sake of ease or acceptance. But each time I honored my boundaries consistently; I reinforced my commitment to myself. This consistency was a form of self-trust, a reminder that I could stand by my values, even when it was challenging.

As I practiced this consistency, I began to feel a greater sense of stability in my life. Boundaries became the foundation upon which I could build a life of peace and authenticity. They provided a framework that allowed me to navigate relationships and experiences with confidence, knowing that I had the tools to protect my well-being. This stability did not mean that life would always be easy or predictable, but it did mean that I could face challenges with a sense of security, knowing that my boundaries were there to support me.

Through this journey, boundaries allowed me to give more freely, not out of obligation but from a place of genuine love and care. When I was not overextended or resentful, I could show up for others with presence and compassion. Boundaries allowed me to engage in relationships from a place of fullness, knowing that I was honoring myself in the process. This balance created a sense of harmony, a reminder that I could care for others without sacrificing my own peace.

Reflecting on the role of boundaries, I felt a deep appreciation for the strength and clarity they brought to my life. Boundaries were not limitations; they were the structure that allowed me to grow, to connect, and to live in alignment with my values. By embracing boundaries, I had created a life that felt true to who I was—a life rooted in respect, empathy, and peace.

Practical Reflections for Strengthening Boundaries

1. **Practice Empathy Through Boundaries**: Honor your own limits and respect others'. Boundaries foster mutual respect and deepen connection in relationships.

2. **Release the Need to Please Everyone**: Choose your well-being over the need for approval. Boundaries reinforce your intrinsic value, independent of others' opinions.

3. **Maintain Consistency in Boundaries**: Reinforce your boundaries with commitment and self-discipline. Consistency builds self-trust and creates a foundation of stability.

As I continued to strengthen my boundaries, I began to see them as essential to self-care. Boundaries allowed me to prioritize my needs and manage my energy, ensuring that I could show up fully in the areas of my life that mattered most. For so long, I had operated from a place of overextension, trying to be everything for everyone. But with boundaries in place, I found the courage to say "no" without guilt, to recognize that my well-being was worthy of my attention. Boundaries became a way to honor my life, to protect the resources that allowed me to be my best self.

One of the most empowering realizations I had was that boundaries allowed me to live with integrity. By defining and honoring my limits, I could make choices that aligned with my values. There were moments when I faced requests or situations that conflicted with my priorities, and in those moments, boundaries gave me a way to act in harmony with myself. I could say "no" or "not now" without feeling that I was letting someone down. This alignment brought a sense of clarity and peace, a reminder that I could live authentically without sacrificing my inner stability.

In embracing boundaries, I also learned the importance of self-compassion. There were times when setting a boundary felt difficult, when I worried about disappointing others or feared judgment. But in those moments, I reminded myself that my boundaries were acts of kindness toward myself. I learned to approach these decisions with gentleness, to release any feelings of guilt or obligation that arose. Self-compassion became a way to reaffirm my worth, a reminder that I deserved to create a life that supported my happiness and well-being.

As I practiced setting boundaries with compassion, they became easier to maintain. Each time I honored a boundary, I reinforced my commitment to myself, creating a cycle of self-respect and self-care. I no longer felt the need to justify my boundaries to others; I understood that they were valid simply because they reflected my needs and values. This understanding brought a sense of freedom, a reminder that I could live authentically without needing approval or permission.

Through this journey, I came to see boundaries as more than just lines—they were expressions of self-love and self-respect. Boundaries allowed me to define my space, to protect my energy, and to nurture my well-being. They were not limitations; they were tools for living in alignment with my values, for engaging with others from a place of wholeness. Boundaries became a way to say, "This is who I am, and this is how I choose to live."

Reflecting on this growth, I felt immense gratitude for the lessons that boundaries had taught me. Boundaries were not easy to establish, but they were worth every effort. They had given me a new sense of peace, a foundation of stability that supported my life in ways I had not anticipated. With boundaries in place, I felt empowered to live fully, to embrace each day with clarity, compassion, and courage. Boundaries were not barriers; they were pathways to a life that felt rich, meaningful, and true.

Key Insights for Practicing Boundaries with Integrity and Compassion

1. **View Boundaries as Acts of Self-Care**: Prioritize your well-being and manage your energy. Boundaries protect the resources that support your best self.

2. **Live with Integrity Through Boundaries**: Make choices that align with your values. Boundaries allow you to act authentically without compromising your inner peace.

3. **Approach Boundaries with Self-Compassion**: Release guilt and embrace kindness toward yourself. Boundaries are valid simply because they reflect your needs and values.

As I reflected on my journey with boundaries, I began to understand that boundaries were not just about saying "no" to others—they were also about saying "yes" to myself. Each time I honored my needs and upheld my limits, I was affirming my own worth, declaring that my well-being mattered. This shift in perspective transformed boundaries from acts of restriction into acts of affirmation. Boundaries allowed me to say "yes" to a life that felt balanced, meaningful, and aligned with my values.

One of the most powerful aspects of boundaries was the way they allowed me to cultivate relationships based on mutual respect. When I communicated my boundaries, I was inviting others to see me as I truly was, to engage with me in a way that honored both my needs and theirs. This honesty created a foundation for deeper, more genuine connections. I found that those who respected my boundaries were those who valued me for who I was, not for what I could provide. This understanding allowed me to nurture relationships that were supportive and empowering, relationships that enhanced my sense of peace.

In my journey, I also learned the importance of practicing boundaries without fear of judgment. There were times when I worried about how others would perceive my boundaries, whether they would view me as selfish or unkind. But I came to realize that the opinions of others did not define my worth or my right to self-care. Boundaries were a personal commitment to my own well-being, a way of living that was true to my needs and values. By releasing the need for external validation, I could embrace boundaries without fear, trusting that those who valued me would understand.

Setting boundaries also taught me that I could navigate conflicts with grace. There were moments when my boundaries clashed with the expectations of others, times when I faced resistance or misunderstanding. But rather than approaching these situations with defensiveness, I learned to communicate calmly and openly, to explain my needs with compassion. This approach allowed me to honor my boundaries while still respecting the perspectives of others. It reminded me that boundaries were not walls but bridges, ways to connect with others in a way that felt healthy and sustainable.

As I continued to integrate boundaries into my life, I felt a profound sense of liberation. Boundaries had given me the freedom to live authentically, to engage in relationships that felt nourishing, and to protect the parts of myself that needed care. They had taught me that I could choose how I wanted to experience the world, that I could create a life that reflected my deepest values. With boundaries in place, I felt empowered to face the future with confidence and peace, knowing that I had the tools to protect my well-being and nurture my growth.

Reflecting on this journey, I felt immense gratitude for the lessons I had learned. Boundaries were more than lines or limits; they were expressions of love, tools for creating a life that was rich, fulfilling, and true to who I was. Boundaries had become an integral part of my healing, a reminder that I could honor myself fully and embrace a life of peace and authenticity.

Guidelines for Embracing Boundaries as Affirmations of Self-Worth

1. **Say "Yes" to Yourself Through Boundaries**: Recognize that boundaries are acts of self-affirmation. Each boundary reflects a commitment to your well-being and values.

2. **Cultivate Respectful Relationships**: Engage with others in a way that honors mutual respect. Boundaries create space for genuine connections based on understanding and support.

3. **Release the Need for Validation**: Embrace boundaries without fear of judgment. Boundaries are a personal commitment to self-care, independent of others' opinions.

CHAPTER 7

Anchoring Empathy: Building Compassionate Connections

As I embarked on the journey of rebuilding trust, I realized that trust was not something that could be rushed or forced. Trust, I came to understand, was a delicate process—a gradual unfolding that required patience, honesty, and a willingness to be vulnerable. For so long, I had held back, protecting myself from the risk of disappointment or betrayal. But as I moved forward, I began to see trust as an essential part of healing, a bridge that connected me not only to others but also to myself.

One of the first steps in rebuilding trust was learning to trust my own judgment. In the past, I had often doubted myself, questioning my perceptions and instincts. But as I delved deeper into this journey, I began to understand that my experiences had given me a unique wisdom—a capacity to discern, to navigate relationships with a sense of self-awareness. Rebuilding trust meant honoring my own intuition, recognizing that my inner voice had value, that it was a guide on which I could rely. This trust in myself became the foundation for everything else, a reminder that I could face the world with confidence and clarity.

In rebuilding trust with myself, I also learned the importance of forgiveness. There were times when I had ignored my instincts, times when I had allowed others to cross boundaries or hurt me. Rebuilding trust required me to forgive myself for these moments, to release the guilt and self-blame that had lingered. This self-forgiveness allowed me to approach my past with compassion, to understand that I had done the best I could with the knowledge and resources I had at the time. By forgiving myself, I created space for growth, a foundation from which I could rebuild with integrity and resilience.

As I strengthened my trust in myself, I found that I could approach relationships with a renewed sense of discernment. Trusting others was not about naivety or blind faith; it was about recognizing when a connection felt safe, when someone's actions aligned with their words. I learned to observe, to allow trust to develop naturally over time rather than forcing it. This discernment allowed me to build relationships that were based on mutual respect and honesty, connections that supported my well-being rather than compromising it.

One of the most profound lessons I learned was that trust was not a guarantee—it was a risk, an act of courage. There were no assurances that others would always meet my expectations or that life would unfold without challenges. But I realized that trust was not about certainty; it was about the willingness to embrace the unknown, to engage with life and relationships despite the risks. This shift in perspective allowed me to release the need for perfect control, to understand that trust was a choice I could make each day, a way of stepping into the world with an open heart.

As I embraced this journey, I began to see trust as an act of self-love. By trusting myself and others, I was allowing myself to experience the richness of connection, the beauty of being fully present in life. Trust became a way to nurture my relationships, to engage with the world from a place of hope rather than fear. It reminded me that, despite past pains, I could still create a life that felt whole and meaningful, a life that reflected my values and aspirations.

Reflecting on this journey, I felt a renewed sense of peace. Trust was not about guarantees or absolutes; it was about choosing to live with openness, to embrace each experience as an opportunity for growth. With trust as my guide, I felt ready to move forward, confident in my ability to navigate life's challenges with courage and grace.

Practical Steps for Rebuilding Trust

1. **Trust Your Own Judgment**: Honor your intuition and recognize the wisdom you hold. Self-trust is the foundation for trusting others.

2. **Forgive Yourself for Past Mistakes**: Release guilt and self-blame, understanding that you did the best you could. Self-forgiveness creates space for growth.

3. **Approach Trust as a Choice, not a Guarantee**: Embrace trust as a way of living with openness and hope. Trusting requires courage and willingness to engage with life.

As I continued the journey of rebuilding trust, I began to appreciate the role of patience. Trust, I learned, could not be rushed, or manufactured; it needed time to grow, like a seed carefully nurtured. In the past, I had often hoped for immediate trust, especially in relationships where I longed for connection. But as I delved deeper, I understood that trust was a gradual process—a journey that required time, experience, and the willingness to be vulnerable. Each small act of honesty, each moment of consistency, added to this foundation, creating a space where trust could flourish naturally.

Patience with others was only one part of the equation; I also had to practice patience with myself. There were moments when I questioned my ability to trust again, moments when fear and doubt crept in. I realized that these feelings were part of the healing process, that trust could not be forced but would emerge in its own time. By accepting this uncertainty with grace, I was able to approach each day with openness, allowing trust to develop organically rather than demanding it from myself or others.

In rebuilding trust, I found the importance of transparency. Trust, I discovered, required a foundation of honesty—a willingness to be open, even when it felt uncomfortable. By sharing my thoughts and feelings honestly, I invited others to do the same, creating an environment of mutual understanding. This transparency was not about revealing everything to everyone; it was about choosing honesty as a guiding principle, a way to foster trust through genuine connection. Transparency allowed me to show up authentically, to build relationships based on respect and truth rather than pretense.

Trust also taught me the value of boundaries. In the past, I had sometimes given trust too freely, hoping that others would meet my expectations. But I learned that trust needed to be balanced with discernment and boundaries.

Setting boundaries allowed me to protect myself while remaining open to connection. I could trust others without compromising my well-being, knowing that boundaries were there to support and protect my heart. This balance created a foundation of trust that felt safe, a reminder that I could engage with others without losing myself in the process.

As I practiced rebuilding trust, forgiveness played an essential role. There were times when trust was broken, times when I faced disappointment or hurt. In these moments, forgiveness allowed me to release the weight of resentment, to move forward without carrying the burdens of the past. Forgiveness did not mean ignoring the pain or pretending that everything was okay; it was a choice to let go, to free myself from the hold that anger and hurt had over me. This forgiveness became an act of self-liberation, a way of clearing space for new experiences and new connections.

Reflecting on this journey, I felt a renewed sense of hope. Trust was no longer a fragile thing, something that could be shattered by a single misstep. Instead, trust became a resilient force within me, a foundation that allowed me to move forward with confidence. Trusting others did not mean expecting perfection; it meant embracing the beauty of connection, knowing that each experience was an opportunity for growth. With trust as my guide, I felt ready to embrace the world with courage, to approach life's uncertainties with a sense of peace and assurance.

Essential Practices for Cultivating Trust

1. **Cultivate Patience in Building Trust**: Allow trust to grow naturally over time. Trust is a journey that requires experience, consistency, and openness.

2. **Embrace Transparency and Honesty**: Build trust through genuine, honest communication. Transparency fosters understanding and mutual respect in relationships.

3. **Balance Trust with Boundaries**: Protect yourself while remaining open. Boundaries create a safe foundation, allowing trust to flourish without compromising one's well-being.

As I delved deeper into the process of rebuilding trust, I began to realize that trust was more than an external act; it was an internal commitment to believe in my capacity to heal and grow. Trust required me to recognize that I had the resilience and wisdom to navigate life's uncertainties, that I could handle disappointment or setbacks without being defined by them. Each time I chose to trust, I was reaffirming my belief in my own strength. This internal commitment became a source of empowerment, a reminder that I could face whatever came my way with confidence and grace.

One of the practices that helped me rebuild trust was mindfulness. By staying present in each moment, I was able to witness my thoughts and emotions without judgment. Mindfulness allowed me to observe the fears or doubts that arose, to recognize them as natural responses rather than signs of weakness. Instead of reacting to these feelings, I learned to breathe through them, to let them pass without allowing them to dictate my choices. This practice became an anchor, a way to remain grounded in the present without being overwhelmed by past hurts or future anxieties.

In rebuilding trust, I also discovered the importance of gratitude. Trust, I realized, was not only about looking forward with hope but also about appreciating the present with gratitude. By focusing on what I valued, on the connections and experiences that enriched my life, I created a foundation of positivity that supported my journey. Gratitude reminded me that trust was not just about others but also about honoring the good in my life. Each moment of gratitude became an affirmation of my ability to see beauty and joy, even during uncertainty.

Another valuable lesson I learned was the importance of celebrating small steps. Trust, I came to understand, was not built on a single leap but through small, consistent actions. Each time I allowed myself to be vulnerable, each moment of honesty or openness added to the foundation of trust. By celebrating these small steps, I acknowledged the progress I was making, the courage it took to rebuild trust piece by piece. This perspective allowed me to approach trust as a journey rather than a destination, to find fulfillment in growth rather than the outcome.

Through this journey, rebuilding trust was an act of courage and compassion. It required me to hold space for my own healing, to approach each day with patience and gentleness. Trust was not about ignoring past pain or pretending that everything was perfect; it was about choosing to move forward with an open heart, to engage with life despite the risks. This openness allowed me to experience life more fully, to embrace connections with authenticity and hope.

Reflecting on this growth, I felt a profound sense of gratitude for the journey I had taken. Trust was no longer a fragile thing, something easily shattered by a single misstep. Instead, it had become a resilient force, a foundation that allowed me to live with confidence and clarity. With trust as my guide, I felt ready to embrace each new experience with courage, to move forward with a heart that was open, strong, and ready for whatever lay ahead.

Steps to Foster Inner Trust and Resilience

1. **Practice Mindfulness to Stay Grounded**: Remain present with your thoughts and emotions. Mindfulness allows you to observe feelings without judgment, supporting a foundation of inner trust.

2. **Cultivate Gratitude as a Foundation for Positivity**: Focus on the positive aspects of your life. Gratitude reinforces your trust in the good and helps you stay open to joy.

3. **Celebrate Small Steps Toward Trust**: Acknowledge each act of courage, each moment of vulnerability. Small steps build a resilient foundation of trust over time.

As I continued rebuilding trust, I realized that trust also required an element of faith. Faith in my own resilience, faith in the goodness of others, and faith in life's unfolding journey. Trust was not about predicting outcomes or controlling the future; it was about embracing the unknown with a sense of hope. By releasing my need for certainty, I allowed trust to become a bridge between the present and the future, a way of engaging with life from a place of openness rather than fear. This faith became a source of strength, a reminder that I could navigate whatever challenges lay ahead.

In this process, I also came to understand the power of vulnerability in building trust. Allowing myself to be vulnerable—whether by expressing my true feelings, sharing my dreams, or acknowledging my fears—was an invitation for others to do the same. Vulnerability became a way to connect authentically, to show up in relationships without the masks or defenses I had once used to protect myself. By embracing vulnerability, I was able to build relationships grounded in honesty and trust, connections that supported my well-being and growth.

One of the most valuable lessons I learned was that trust could coexist with caution. Trusting did not mean ignoring red flags or overlooking behaviors that caused discomfort. It meant approaching relationships with a balance of openness and discernment, allowing trust to develop naturally rather than rushing into it. This balance gave me the freedom to engage with others while still honoring my own boundaries. By trusting cautiously, I could protect my heart without closing it off completely, creating a safe space for connection without compromising my peace.

In rebuilding trust, I also found the importance of resilience. Trusting others and life itself was not without its risks; there were times when trust was tested, moments when I faced disappointment or setbacks. But each time I chose to trust again, I strengthened my capacity to bounce back, to approach each experience with a fresh perspective. Resilience allowed me to move forward without being weighed down by past hurts, to see each relationship and opportunity as unique rather than influenced by old wounds. This resilience became the foundation of my trust, a reminder that I could face whatever came my way with courage.

Reflecting on this journey, I felt a profound sense of freedom. Trust was no longer something I granted blindly;

it was a conscious choice, a way of living that allowed me to engage with life fully. Trusting did not mean that life would be without challenges; it meant that I could face those challenges with a heart open to growth, with a willingness to embrace each experience as an opportunity for healing and connection. Trust had become a path to peace, a way of living that allowed me to create a life filled with meaning, hope, and resilience.

As I embraced this new understanding of trust, I felt a renewed sense of joy and purpose. Trust was no longer a fragile thing, easily broken by disappointment or doubt. It was a powerful force, a foundation that allowed me to move forward with clarity and strength. With trust as my guide, I felt ready to embrace each new chapter of life, to approach the future with a heart that was open, whole, and ready for whatever lay ahead.

Key Principles for Building Resilient Trust

1. **Embrace Faith in Life's Journey**: Release the need for certainty and approach life with hope. Faith in the unknown strengthens your capacity for trust.

2. **Practice Vulnerability as a Foundation for Connection**: Show up authentically in relationships. Vulnerability fosters genuine connections built on honesty and trust.

3. **Balance Trust with Caution and Resilience**: Approach trust with openness and discernment. Resilience allows you to face challenges without being defined by past hurts.

As I reflected on this journey of trust, I realized that trust was a gift I gave to myself. Trusting allowed me to experience life fully, to engage with the world with an open heart, unburdened by fear. Each act of trust, each moment of vulnerability, was a declaration of my willingness to live with hope rather than reservation. Trust was not a guarantee of a perfect outcome; it was a commitment to embrace life's possibilities, to step into each moment with courage and resilience.

This journey taught me that trust was also a way of honoring the present. By choosing to trust, I was choosing to live fully in each moment, to engage with others without the weight of past hurts or the fear of future disappointments. Trust allowed me to be present in my relationships, to listen with empathy, and to connect with others on a deeper level. It reminded me that each moment was unique, a chance to create new memories and connections, free from the constraints of what had been.

In this process, trust requires self-compassion. There were times when doubts resurfaced, moments when fear or insecurity would creep back in. But I learned to approach these feelings with gentleness, to remind myself that trust was not a linear path. Some days would feel easier than others, and that was okay. Self-compassion allowed me to navigate these moments with grace, to trust that I was doing the best I could. This kindness toward myself became a foundation for growth, a reminder that I was worthy of the peace and freedom that trust brought.

Rebuilding trust also taught me the importance of celebrating progress. Each step I took, each moment of openness, was a testament to the strength and resilience I had cultivated. By acknowledging this growth, I reinforced my commitment to trust, reminding myself of how far I had come. Celebrating progress became a way of honoring my journey, a way of affirming that I could create a life rooted in hope and connection.

As I moved forward, I felt a renewed sense of gratitude for this journey. Trust was no longer something I feared or withheld; it was a source of strength, a foundation that allowed me to embrace life with courage. I understood that trust was a continuous choice, a way of engaging with each new experience with an open heart. Trust had transformed from a fragile thing into a powerful force within me, a reminder that I could live fully, love deeply, and face whatever came my way with confidence.

With trust as my guide, I felt ready to step into the future, to approach life with a sense of peace and joy. Trust was not the absence of fear; it was the courage to move forward despite it, to choose connection over isolation, hope over hesitation. Trust had become a gift I carried with me, a reminder of the beauty and resilience that defined my journey. As I embraced this gift, I knew that I was ready for whatever life had in store, ready to create a life that was rich, meaningful, and true to who I was.

Foundations for Living a Life Rooted in Trust

1. **Honor the Present with Trust**: Engage fully in each moment without the weight of the past. Trust allows you to experience life with an open heart.

2. **Practice Self-Compassion on the Journey of Trust**: Approach doubts and insecurities with kindness. Self-compassion supports resilience and growth in the process of trusting.

3. **Celebrate Each Step of Progress**: Acknowledge your growth and commitment to trust. Celebrating progress affirms your journey and strengthens your foundation of trust.

CHAPTER 8

Anchoring Resilience: A Foundation for Growth

As I began to reflect on the concept of resilience, I realized that resilience was more than just the ability to "bounce back" after hardship. Resilience was a profound inner strength, a commitment to growth, and a willingness to adapt. It was the quiet courage that allowed me to face each day, even in the face of uncertainty or pain. Resilience was not about avoiding challenges or pretending that everything was fine; it was about finding the strength to keep going, to embrace life with all its ups and downs, and to grow through each experience.

One of the first steps in embracing resilience was accepting that challenges were a natural part of life. For so long, I had resisted pain, hoping to avoid difficulty and maintain a sense of control. But as I moved forward, I began to see challenges as opportunities for growth, as experiences that shaped and strengthened me. Embracing resilience meant letting go of the need to control every outcome, trusting that I had the capacity to navigate whatever came my way. This acceptance allowed me to approach life with openness, a willingness to learn, and a belief that I could grow through each experience.

In this journey, I learned that resilience was also about finding meaning in adversity. Each challenge, each setback, taught me something valuable—about myself, about life, and about what truly mattered. By looking for meaning in difficult experiences, I was able to transform pain into wisdom, to find purpose in situations that once felt overwhelming. This shift in perspective gave me the strength to keep going, a reminder that even the most difficult moments held lessons that could serve my growth.

Practicing resilience also required me to cultivate patience. Resilience was not an instant fix or a quick solution; it was a gradual process, a journey that unfolded over time. There were days when resilience felt effortless when I moved through challenges with ease. And then there were days when resilience felt like a struggle, when each step forward felt heavy and difficult. By embracing patience, I was able to honor this process, to understand that resilience would grow stronger with each experience. This patience allowed me to approach life with gentleness, to trust that each moment, no matter how challenging, was part of my journey.

As I embraced resilience, it also required self-compassion. There were moments when I stumbled, times when I felt overwhelmed or discouraged. But instead of judging myself for these feelings, I learned to approach them with kindness, to understand that resilience was not about being invulnerable but about being gentle with myself through life's challenges. Self-compassion allowed me to face each difficulty with grace, to trust that I was doing the best I could, and to recognize that resilience was a journey, not a destination.

Reflecting on this journey, I felt a profound sense of gratitude for the strength that resilience had given me. Resilience was not something I had to "earn" or prove; it was a gift within me, a source of inner power that allowed me to navigate life's challenges with courage and hope. By embracing resilience, I was able to create a life that felt rich and meaningful, a life that honored both my strength and my vulnerability. Resilience became a foundation for everything else—a reminder that, no matter what happened, I had the power to face it with courage, grace, and an open heart.

Practical Steps for Building Resilience

1. **Accept Challenges as Part of Life's Journey:** Embrace difficulties as opportunities for growth. Acceptance allows you to approach life with openness and strength.
2. **Find Meaning in Adversity:** Look for the lessons in each challenge. Transform pain into wisdom by finding purpose in difficult experiences.
3. **Cultivate Patience and Self-Compassion:** Honor resilience as a gradual process. Approach each moment with gentleness, trusting that resilience will grow over time.

As I continued to explore resilience, I discovered that resilience was not only about adapting but also about building a foundation of inner strength. This foundation allowed me to face challenges with confidence, knowing that I had cultivated the tools and mindset needed to navigate life's uncertainties. Resilience became a way of grounding myself, a reminder that I could approach each experience with courage and trust in my ability to overcome obstacles. By strengthening this inner foundation, I found a sense of stability that supported me even in the most turbulent times.

One of the most transformative aspects of resilience was the ability to reframe difficult situations. Instead of viewing challenges as setbacks, I began to see them as opportunities for growth and self-discovery. Reframing allowed me to approach each experience with curiosity, to ask myself, "What can I learn from this? How can this experience serve my growth?" This shift in perspective was empowering; it reminded me that I was not a victim of my circumstances but an active participant in my own journey of growth. By choosing to see challenges in this way, I transformed adversity into a source of strength and wisdom.

Resilience also required me to develop a sense of adaptability. Life, I learned, was rarely predictable or linear. There were twists and turns, unexpected events, and moments of change that I could not control. But by cultivating adaptability, I was able to approach these changes with openness, to embrace the unknown rather than resist it. Adaptability became a way of flowing with life, a reminder that I could face each new situation with flexibility and a willingness to learn. This adaptability allowed me to maintain my peace, to understand that resilience was not about rigidly holding on but about gracefully letting go when necessary.

Through this journey, resilience was deeply connected to hope. Hope was the light that guided me through the darkest moments, a reminder that no matter how challenging things might seem, there was always a possibility for something better. By holding on to hope, I was able to keep moving forward, to believe in my capacity to overcome and to trust that each difficulty held the potential for growth. Hope became a companion to resilience, a source of motivation that fueled my journey and reminded me that each moment held the promise of new possibilities.

As I practiced resilience, I also learned the importance of surrounding myself with supportive relationships. Resilience was not something I had to cultivate alone; it was strengthened by the encouragement and understanding of others. By connecting with people who valued my growth, who offered support without judgment, I found a sense of community that uplifted me. These relationships became sources of strength, a reminder that resilience was not just an individual journey but a shared experience that flourished through connection and empathy.

Reflecting on this journey, I felt immense gratitude for the strength that resilience had brought into my life. Resilience was no longer something I had to struggle to maintain; it had become a natural part of who I was, a foundation that allowed me to face each new day with courage and hope. By embracing resilience, I was able to create a life that felt purposeful and fulfilling, a life that honored my capacity for growth and transformation.

Key Practices for Cultivating Resilience

1. **Reframe Challenges as Opportunities for Growth**: Shift your perspective to see adversity as a chance for self-discovery. Reframing empowers you to take an active role in your journey.

2. **Develop Adaptability to Embrace Change**: Cultivate flexibility to face life's uncertainties. Adaptability allows you to flow with life rather than resist it.

3. **Nurture Hope as a Source of Motivation**: Hold on to hope during challenging times. Hope fuels resilience, reminding you of life's endless possibilities.

As I deepened my understanding of resilience, I came to realize that resilience was not just an individual pursuit; it was also about finding strength in community. Surrounding myself with people who understood and supported my journey became a powerful source of resilience. These connections provided a safe space where I could share my experiences, receive encouragement, and feel a sense of belonging. By opening up to others, I discovered that resilience could flourish through connection, that shared strength was a profound source of comfort and empowerment.

Building a supportive community required me to be intentional about the people I allowed into my life. I learned to seek relationships that were rooted in empathy and mutual respect, connections where I could both give and receive support. This approach allowed me to create a network of relationships that uplifted me, reminding me that I was not alone in my journey. These relationships became a foundation of resilience, a reminder that while

I could face challenges on my own, I could also lean on others when needed.

Resilience also taught me the importance of self-reflection. By taking time to reflect on my experiences, I was able to gain insights into my patterns, strengths, and areas for growth. Self-reflection allowed me to approach each challenge with a sense of curiosity, to ask myself what I could learn and how I could grow. This practice became a way of integrating each experience into my journey, transforming setbacks into valuable lessons. Self-reflection strengthened my resilience by allowing me to approach life with a mindset of continuous growth and self-discovery.

One of the most transformative aspects of resilience was the realization that resilience was not about perfection. There were times when I stumbled, moments when I felt overwhelmed or discouraged. But I learned that resilience was about persistence, about choosing to get back up each time I fell. This acceptance allowed me to release the pressure of needing to be strong all the time, to understand that resilience included moments of vulnerability and struggle. By embracing imperfection, I was able to cultivate a resilience that was rooted in authenticity rather than in unrealistic expectations.

Resilience also helped me cultivate a sense of gratitude. Each time I overcame a challenge; each moment of growth became a reminder of the strength and grace that I had developed. Gratitude allowed me to recognize and honor my progress, to appreciate the journey I had taken and the resilience I had built along the way. This sense of gratitude created a positive foundation for my life, a reminder that even the most difficult experiences had contributed to my growth and transformation.

Reflecting on this journey, I felt a deep sense of peace. Resilience was no longer something I struggled to maintain; it had become a natural part of who I was. Each experience, each challenge, had strengthened my capacity to face life with courage, hope, and gratitude. By embracing resilience, I was able to create a life that felt grounded, meaningful, and true to who I was. Resilience had given me the strength to navigate life's uncertainties, a foundation that allowed me to move forward with confidence and clarity.

Guiding Principles for Embracing Resilience

1. **Find Strength in Community**: Surround yourself with supportive relationships. Connection allows resilience to flourish through shared strength and encouragement.

2. **Embrace Self-Reflection as a Tool for Growth**: Reflect on your experiences to gain insights and foster continuous growth. Self-reflection transforms setbacks into valuable lessons.

3. **Cultivate Gratitude for Each Step of Progress**: Honor your journey and the resilience you have built. Gratitude reinforces a positive foundation, reminding you of the strength you have gained.

As I continued to build resilience, I realized that resilience was also about cultivating a sense of purpose. Having a purpose—a sense of direction or meaning—allowed me to navigate life's challenges with a renewed sense of motivation. Purpose gave me something to hold on to, a reason to keep moving forward even in challenging times. Whether it was a personal goal, a desire to make a difference, or simply the commitment to live with integrity, purpose became a guiding light that strengthened my resilience and fueled my determination.

In my journey, resilience also required me to stay open to new possibilities. There were moments when I faced unexpected changes, times when life took a direction for which I had not planned. Instead of resisting these changes, I learned to embrace them, to see each new possibility as an opportunity for growth. This openness allowed me to adapt to life's twists and turns, to approach each experience with curiosity rather than fear. By staying open to the unknown, resilience became a source of excitement rather than anxiety, a reminder that life held endless potential.

Resilience also taught me the importance of self-care. Taking care of myself—physically, mentally, and emotionally—

became a way of nurturing the resilience within me. Self-care allowed me to recharge, to approach each day with a renewed sense of strength and focus. It reminded me that resilience was not just about pushing through challenges but also about taking time to rest, to honor my needs, and to replenish my energy. By prioritizing self-care, I was able to build a resilience that was sustainable, one that supported my well-being in both the highs and lows of life.

As I embraced resilience, it also required me to let go of the need for perfection. There were times when I set high expectations for myself, moments when I felt disappointed by my own perceived shortcomings. But resilience taught me that I did not have to be perfect to be strong. Resilience was about showing up as I was, about embracing both my strengths and my vulnerabilities. This acceptance allowed me to approach life with authenticity, to understand that resilience was a journey, not a measure of flawlessness.

Reflecting on this journey, I felt a profound sense of gratitude for the resilience that had carried me through. Resilience was no longer something I had to prove; it was a natural part of who I was, a foundation that allowed me to live with confidence, hope, and joy. By embracing resilience, I had found the strength to face life's challenges with an open heart, to approach each day with a sense of purpose and possibility. Resilience had become more than just a skill; it had become a way of life, a reminder that I could thrive, grow, and create meaning no matter what I encountered.

This journey of resilience had transformed me in ways I had not anticipated. It had shown me the power of acceptance, the beauty of adaptability, and the importance of self-compassion. With resilience as my guide, I felt ready to face the future with courage and peace, knowing that I had the strength to overcome whatever came my way. Resilience was a gift I carried within me, a foundation that would support me through all of life's journeys, a reminder that I could live fully, deeply, and with unwavering hope.

Practices for Cultivating a Resilient Mindset

1. **Define and Pursue Your Purpose**: Find a sense of meaning that motivates you. Purpose strengthens resilience, giving you direction through life's challenges.

2. **Stay Open to New Possibilities**: Embrace life's changes with curiosity. Openness allows resilience to become a source of excitement rather than fear.

3. **Prioritize Self-Care for Sustained Resilience**: Take time to rest and recharge. Self-care nurtures resilience, supporting you through both highs and lows.

As I reached a deeper understanding of resilience, I realized that resilience was more than a response to hardship; it was a way of living that allowed me to embrace each day with hope and confidence. Resilience became a steady force within me, a foundation that supported me through all of life's changes. It was the quiet assurance that I could face each challenge with grace, knowing that my strength did not depend on the absence of struggle but on my commitment to growth and renewal. By embracing resilience as a way of life, I found a sense of peace that transcended any single experience or outcome.

One of the most valuable lessons I learned was that resilience was not something that could be perfected or fully "achieved." Resilience was an ongoing journey, a continuous process of learning, adapting, and growing. There were moments when resilience felt effortless when I moved through challenges with ease and confidence. And then there were times when resilience felt challenging, when I needed to remind myself of the strength I had cultivated. By accepting resilience as a journey rather than a destination, I was able to approach each day with patience and compassion, knowing that each moment was an opportunity to grow stronger.

In embracing resilience, I also learned the importance of letting go. There were situations, relationships, and expectations that I had once held tightly, moments when I struggled to accept change. But resilience taught me that letting go was not a sign of weakness; it was an act of self-respect and trust. Letting go allowed me to release what no longer served me, to create space for new experiences and opportunities. This ability to let go became a powerful aspect of resilience, a reminder that I could move forward with an open heart, free from the weight of the past.

Reflecting on this journey, I felt immense gratitude for the resilience that had become an integral part of who I was. Resilience had given me the courage to live authentically, to approach each experience with a sense of hope and purpose. It showed me that I could face life's challenges with grace and find strength even in the most difficult moments. By embracing resilience, I had created a life that felt true to who I was, a life that honored both my strengths and my vulnerabilities.

This journey of resilience had transformed me in ways I had not anticipated. It had shown me the power of acceptance, the beauty of adaptability, and the importance of self-compassion. With resilience as my guide, I felt ready to face the future with courage and peace, knowing that I had the strength to overcome whatever came my way. Resilience was a gift I carried within me, a foundation that would support me through all of life's journeys, a reminder that I could live fully, deeply, and with unwavering hope.

As I moved forward, I carried this resilience with me, a source of strength and inspiration. Resilience had become more than a response to life's challenges; it had become a way of living that allowed me to embrace each day with joy, purpose, and hope. By embracing resilience, I had created a life that felt rich, meaningful, and true—a life that honored both my journey and the strength that defined it.

Final Reflections on Embracing Resilience

1. **Embrace Resilience as a Way of Life**: Allow resilience to be a continuous journey of growth and renewal. Resilience is a way of living that empowers you to face each day with hope.

2. **Practice Letting Go to Create Space for Growth**: Release what no longer serves you. Letting go supports resilience by allowing you to move forward with freedom and openness.

3. **Approach Each Moment as an Opportunity for Strength**: Recognize resilience as an ongoing process. Each experience is a chance to grow stronger and live authentically.

CHAPTER 9

Navigating Forgiveness: Letting Go to Heal

As I began to explore forgiveness, I realized that forgiveness was more than an act of releasing others; it was a profound gift I could give myself. Forgiveness allowed me to free my heart from the weight of resentment, to create space for peace, and to embrace life without the burdens of the past. For so long, I had held onto feelings of hurt and anger, hoping that these emotions would somehow protect me from being hurt again. But as I moved forward, I came to understand that forgiveness was not about excusing what had happened—it was about releasing myself from the grip of pain.

One of the first steps in embracing forgiveness was accepting that forgiveness was a choice I could make for my own healing. Forgiveness did not mean that I had to forget or condone what had happened; it simply meant that I could choose to let go of the emotional hold that the past had on me. This choice allowed me to reclaim my sense of peace, to focus on my present and future rather than being tethered to old wounds. By choosing forgiveness, I was giving myself permission to move forward, to live with a heart that was open and free.

In this journey, I discovered that forgiveness required me to embrace empathy. There were times when I struggled to let go, moments when resentment felt justified. But by approaching these feelings with empathy—by considering the experiences and struggles of those involved—I was able to soften my perspective. Empathy allowed me to see beyond my own hurt, to recognize that everyone carried their own wounds and challenges. This understanding did not excuse hurtful actions, but it allowed me to release the need for retribution, to see forgiveness as an act of compassion that served my own peace.

Forgiveness also taught me the importance of setting healthy boundaries. Forgiving did not mean allowing others to hurt me repeatedly; it meant finding a way to release the past while still honoring my own well-being. Boundaries allowed me to protect myself without carrying the weight of anger or resentment. They became a way to create healthy connections, to engage with others from a place of respect and self-worth. By setting boundaries, I was able to forgive without sacrificing my peace, to approach relationships with clarity and confidence.

Through this journey, I learned that forgiveness was a process. There were days when forgiveness felt easy, when I could let go with a sense of peace. And then there were days when old feelings resurfaced, when hurt and anger returned. Instead of judging myself for these moments, I learned to approach them with patience, to understand that forgiveness was not a one-time event but an ongoing journey. This patience allowed me to move forward with grace, to trust that each moment of forgiveness was a step toward freedom.

Reflecting on this journey, I felt a profound sense of peace. Forgiveness had given me the courage to release what no longer served me, to live with a heart that was unburdened by past hurts. By embracing forgiveness, I was able to create a life that felt whole and meaningful, a life that honored my growth and resilience. Forgiveness was not something I did for others; it was a gift I gave to myself—a way of living that allowed me to approach each day with hope, peace, and an open heart.

▌ Practical Steps for Embracing Forgiveness

1. **Choose Forgiveness for Your Own Peace:** Release the hold that the past has on you. Forgiveness is a choice that allows you to live freely in the present.

2. **Practice Empathy to Soften Resentment:** Approach hurtful experiences with compassion. Empathy helps you release anger and fosters a sense of understanding.

3. **Set Boundaries to Protect Your Peace:** Forgive without compromising your well-being. Boundaries support forgiveness by honoring your needs and self-respect.

As I continued to explore forgiveness, I began to understand that forgiveness was also about self-forgiveness. For so long, I had carried feelings of guilt and regret, moments from the past that lingered in my mind. I realized that self-forgiveness was essential to moving forward, to embracing life with an open heart. Just as I had chosen to forgive others, I could also choose to forgive myself, to release the judgments I held against myself. This self-forgiveness became a way of acknowledging my own humanity, a reminder that I, too, deserved grace and compassion.

One of the most powerful aspects of self-forgiveness was learning to view my past mistakes as lessons rather than failures. Each mistake, each moment of imperfection, had taught me something valuable—about myself, about life, and about what truly mattered. By seeing these moments as opportunities for growth, I was able to release the shame and self-blame that had held me back. Self-forgiveness allowed me to approach my past with understanding rather than judgment, to honor my journey without being defined by it.

In practicing self-forgiveness, I also learned the importance of self-compassion. There were times when old feelings of guilt or regret would resurface, moments when I felt unworthy of the peace I was seeking. But by approaching these feelings with gentleness, by reminding myself that I was doing the best I could, I was able to navigate these moments with grace. Self-compassion became a foundation for self-forgiveness, a reminder that I could be both accountable and kind toward myself. This kindness allowed me to move forward with confidence, to trust that I was worthy of the peace and healing I sought.

Forgiveness, I found, also required me to release expectations. There were times when I had hoped for an apology or acknowledgment from others, moments when forgiveness depended on external validation. But as I moved deeper into this journey, I understood that forgiveness was a personal decision, one that did not rely on others' actions. Releasing expectations allowed me to reclaim my own power, to forgive for my own peace rather than waiting for others to meet my needs. This release became a liberating act, a reminder that forgiveness was within my control.

Through this journey, I learned that forgiveness was not about absolving others or denying my own pain; it was about choosing freedom over resentment. Each time I forgave, I felt a renewed sense of peace, a reminder that I was not defined by my past or by the actions of others. Forgiveness became a way of creating space for joy, of allowing myself to live without the burdens that had once held me back. This choice to forgive allowed me to approach life with a sense of lightness, a heart that was open to the beauty of each moment.

Reflecting on this journey, I felt immense gratitude for the freedom that forgiveness had brought into my life. Forgiveness was no longer something I struggled with; it had become a source of strength, a foundation that allowed me to live fully and authentically. By embracing forgiveness, I had created a life that felt grounded and meaningful, a life that honored both my journey and the strength it had taken to let go. Forgiveness was not an endpoint; it was a way of living that allowed me to embrace each day with hope, peace, and an unwavering commitment to my own well-being.

Steps to Embrace Self-Forgiveness and Release Expectations

1. **View Mistakes as Opportunities for Growth**: Shift your perspective on past mistakes. Self-forgiveness allows you to honor your journey without self-blame.

2. **Cultivate Self-Compassion on the Path to Peace**: Approach feelings of guilt with gentleness. Self-compassion supports your journey toward self-forgiveness and healing.

3. **Release Expectations for True Freedom**: Forgive for your own peace, independent of others' actions. Releasing expectations empowers you to reclaim your own well-being.

As I continued to deepen my understanding of forgiveness, I came to realize that forgiveness was not just about releasing others or myself from the past. Forgiveness was about reclaiming my energy, redirecting it toward healing and growth rather than letting it be consumed by anger or regret. Each time I chose to forgive, I felt a sense of freedom—a lightness that allowed me to engage with life more fully. Forgiveness became a practice of self-liberation, a way of clearing the emotional space I needed to thrive.

One of the most transformative aspects of forgiveness was learning to forgive without conditions. In the past, I had sometimes placed conditions on forgiveness, feeling that it depended on an apology or acknowledgment from others. But as I embraced forgiveness more deeply, I understood that true forgiveness was unconditional; it was a gift I gave to myself, independent of what others did or did not do. This shift allowed me to approach forgiveness from a place of personal empowerment, to release the need for external validation and find peace within.

In embracing forgiveness, I also learned the importance of mindfulness. There were moments when old feelings would resurface, times when anger or hurt would return unexpectedly. Instead of resisting these feelings, I learned to observe them mindfully, to allow them to arise without letting them control me. Mindfulness allowed me to acknowledge my emotions without being overwhelmed by them, to approach each feeling with a sense of curiosity and acceptance. This practice became a foundation for forgiveness, a way of honoring my emotional journey without becoming stuck in it.

Forgiveness also taught me the value of resilience. Choosing to forgive, especially in challenging situations, required strength and perseverance. There were days when forgiveness felt like a struggle, moments when it felt easier to hold onto resentment. But each time I chose forgiveness, I strengthened my resilience, building the emotional fortitude to face future challenges with grace. Resilience allowed me to approach forgiveness not as a one-time event but as a practice that would support me throughout my life. This resilience became a reminder that I was capable of healing, that I could face each experience with courage and peace.

Through this journey, forgiveness was a way of honoring my own journey. By releasing the past, I was able to create space for joy, growth, and new experiences. Forgiveness became a reminder that I was not defined by what had happened to me or by the actions of others. It was a choice to embrace my own story with compassion, to see each experience as part of a journey that had shaped me into who I was. This sense of ownership allowed me to live more authentically, to engage with life from a place of wholeness and strength.

Reflecting on this journey, I felt immense gratitude for the peace that forgiveness had brought into my life. Forgiveness was no longer something I approached with reluctance; it had become a practice that allowed me to live with an open heart, free from the burdens of the past. By embracing forgiveness, I had found a sense of inner freedom—a foundation that allowed me to approach each day with hope, purpose, and a deep sense of peace.

Key Practices for Embracing Forgiveness as a Path to Freedom

1. **Forgive Without Conditions for True Peace**: Release the need for validation or acknowledgment from others. Unconditional forgiveness empowers you to reclaim your own peace.

2. **Practice Mindfulness to Honor Your Emotional Journey**: Allow emotions to arise without judgment. Mindfulness supports forgiveness by helping you observe emotions without becoming overwhelmed.

3. **Cultivate Resilience Through Forgiveness**: Approach forgiveness as a continuous practice. Resilience builds emotional fortitude, allowing you to face future challenges with strength.

As I delved further into the process of forgiveness, I began to understand that forgiveness also required courage. Each time I chose to forgive, I stepped into a place of vulnerability, opening my heart to healing. It took courage to let go of familiar feelings of resentment, to release the comfort of justified anger and step into the unknown territory of peace. This courage was not about ignoring my pain or pretending that everything was okay; it was about choosing freedom, about allowing myself to move forward without the constraints of past hurts.

In practicing forgiveness, I learned that it was essential to separate forgiveness from reconciliation. There were relationships in my life where reconciliation was not possible or healthy, connections where boundaries were necessary to protect my well-being. Forgiveness did not mean reestablishing these connections; it meant releasing the emotional hold these relationships had on me. By understanding this distinction, I was able to forgive without compromising my peace, to honor my own healing while respecting the boundaries that supported it.

Forgiveness also taught me the value of self-empowerment. Each time I chose to forgive, I was reclaiming my power, taking ownership of my emotional journey. Forgiveness allowed me to make peace with the past on my own terms, to find closure without relying on others. This empowerment became a source of strength, a reminder that I could create my own peace, independent of external circumstances. By embracing forgiveness, I was able to approach life with a sense of autonomy and confidence, knowing that I could choose how I wanted to engage with my own story.

Through this journey, forgiveness was deeply connected to acceptance. Forgiving did not mean changing what had happened or ignoring the impact of certain experiences; it meant accepting reality as it was, without resistance. This acceptance allowed me to let go of the "what-ifs" and "should-haves," to focus on what was within my control. By embracing acceptance, I was able to find peace in the present, to release the desire to change the past and focus on creating a fulfilling future.

Reflecting on this journey, I felt immense gratitude for the freedom that forgiveness had brought into my life. Forgiveness had allowed me to create a life that felt rich and meaningful, a life that honored my resilience and growth. It had shown me the power of courage, the beauty of acceptance, and the strength of self-empowerment. By embracing forgiveness, I was able to live with a heart that was open, unburdened by past hurts, and ready for the beauty of each new moment.

As I moved forward, I carried this forgiveness with me as a foundation for peace. Forgiveness had become more than just a response to past pain; it had become a way of living, a practice that allowed me to approach each day with clarity and grace. By choosing forgiveness, I had created a life that felt whole and true, a life that reflected both my strength and my compassion.

Principles for Forgiving with Courage and Acceptance

1. **Embrace Courage to Choose Forgiveness**: Recognize that forgiveness is an act of courage. Forgiveness frees you from the past, allowing you to move forward with peace.

2. **Separate Forgiveness from Reconciliation**: Honor boundaries in relationships where needed. Forgiveness does not require reconciliation, allowing you to prioritize your well-being.

3. **Empower Yourself by Accepting Reality**: Release resistance and accept what is. Acceptance supports forgiveness by grounding you in the present and allowing you to let go of the past.

As I reflected on the journey of forgiveness, I realized that forgiveness was about creating space for inner peace. Each time I chose to forgive, I was choosing to free myself from the burdens of anger, resentment, and regret. Forgiveness allowed me to live more fully in the present, to experience life with an open heart rather than a guarded one. This sense of peace became a foundation for everything else, a reminder that I could face the future without carrying the weight of the past.

One of the most profound lessons I learned was that forgiveness was a daily choice. There were times when old feelings resurfaced, moments when anger or hurt would return unexpectedly. But by approaching forgiveness as a continuous practice, I was able to release these feelings with compassion rather than frustration. This daily commitment to forgiveness allowed me to maintain a sense of peace, to remind myself that forgiveness was not a single act but a way of life.

Forgiveness also taught me the value of gratitude. Each time I let go of past hurts, I felt a renewed appreciation for the present. By releasing the past, I was able to see the beauty of each moment, to approach life with a heart that was open to joy. Gratitude became a natural extension of forgiveness, a way of honoring the journey I had taken and the strength I had found within myself. This gratitude allowed me to create a life that felt meaningful, a life that reflected both my growth and my resilience.

In embracing forgiveness, I also learned to trust myself. Forgiving did not mean ignoring my own needs or boundaries; it meant trusting my ability to create a life that felt whole and balanced. This trust allowed me to approach forgiveness with confidence, to know that I could release the past without compromising my well-being. By trusting myself, I was able to forgive from a place of strength, to create relationships and experiences that honored my own journey.

Reflecting on this journey, I felt immense gratitude for the peace that forgiveness had brought into my life. Forgiveness had allowed me to create a life that felt true to who I was, a life that honored my strength, my compassion, and my resilience. By embracing forgiveness, I was able to live with an open heart, to experience the fullness of life without the constraints of past pain. Forgiveness had become more than just a response to hardship; it had become a way of living that allowed me to approach each day with hope, peace, and a deep sense of joy.

As I moved forward, I carried this forgiveness with me as a foundation for all that was to come. Forgiveness had given me the freedom to live authentically, to engage with life from a place of wholeness and love. By choosing forgiveness, I had created a life that felt rich, meaningful, and true—a life that reflected both my journey and the strength it had taken to let go.

Foundational Principles for a Life Rooted in Forgiveness

1. **Embrace Forgiveness as a Daily Choice**: Release past hurts regularly. Forgiveness is a continuous practice that supports peace and emotional freedom.

2. **Cultivate Gratitude as a Partner to Forgiveness**: Appreciate the present with an open heart. Gratitude honors your journey and allows you to live fully in each moment.

3. **Trust Yourself to Forgive with Confidence**:
    Approach forgiveness from a place of strength.
    Self-trust empowers you to release the past
    without compromising your well-being.

CHAPTER 10

Anchored Authenticity: Living True to Yourself

As I began to embrace the idea of living authentically, I realized that authenticity was more than simply being true to myself; it was a commitment to live in alignment with the values and lessons I had cultivated throughout my journey. Living authentically allowed me to approach each day with a sense of peace, knowing that I was honoring the person I had become. This authenticity became a foundation for my life, a reminder that I could live with integrity, guided by the strength and resilience I had developed.

One of the first steps in living authentically was learning to trust my inner voice. For so long, I had looked to others for validation, seeking approval or guidance outside of myself.

But as I moved forward, I understood that true authenticity meant listening to my own needs, desires, and values. By trusting my inner voice, I was able to make decisions that felt aligned with my truth, to navigate life with a sense of clarity and confidence. This trust became a source of empowerment, a reminder that I could create a life that felt whole and meaningful.

In embracing authenticity, I also learned the importance of honoring my boundaries. Boundaries were not just about protecting myself from harm; they were a way of respecting my own journey, of ensuring that I could engage with others from a place of wholeness. By setting and maintaining boundaries, I was able to create relationships that felt balanced and fulfilling, connections where I could give without losing myself. This approach allowed me to engage with the world without compromising my peace, to create a life that felt true to who I was.

Living authentically also required me to embrace vulnerability. There were moments when being true to myself meant taking risks, moments when authenticity felt both exhilarating and frightening. But by allowing myself to be vulnerable, I was able to experience life more fully, to engage with others in meaningful ways. Vulnerability became a way of showing up authentically, of expressing my true self without fear of judgment. This openness allowed me to build deeper connections, to create a life filled with relationships that were grounded in trust and mutual respect.

Reflecting on this journey, I felt a deep sense of gratitude for the freedom that authenticity had brought into my life. Living authentically had allowed me to release the expectations of others, to live with a heart that was open and unburdened. By embracing my true self, I created a life that felt purposeful and fulfilling, a life that reflected both my strength and compassion. This authenticity became a foundation for everything else, a reminder that I could approach each day with peace and joy.

As I moved forward, I carried this authenticity with me as a foundation for all that was to come. Living authentically allowed me to create a life that felt rich and meaningful, a life that honored both my journey and the values I had embraced. By choosing authenticity, I was able to approach each new experience with hope, courage, and a heart that was open to the beauty of each moment.

Key Practices for Living Authentically

1. **Trust Your Inner Voice as a Source of Guidance**: Listen to your own needs and values. Self-trust allows you to make decisions aligned with your truth.

2. **Honor Boundaries to Protect Your Peace**: Set boundaries that reflect your needs. Boundaries

support authenticity by allowing you to engage without compromising your well-being.

3. **Embrace Vulnerability for Deeper Connections**: Show up as your true self in relationships. Vulnerability fosters authentic connections grounded in trust.

As I continued to explore what it meant to live authentically, I realized that authenticity was deeply connected to embracing my own growth. Living authentically was not about achieving a fixed version of myself but rather about allowing myself the freedom to evolve. Each day, each new experience, was an opportunity to learn, to expand, and to deepen my understanding of who I was becoming. Embracing growth allowed me to approach life with curiosity, to engage with each moment as an opportunity to build a life that felt aligned with my evolving self.

In this journey, I also learned the importance of self-compassion. There were times when I struggled with doubts, moments when I felt that I had not lived up to my own expectations. But by practicing self-compassion, I was able to approach these feelings with kindness, to remind myself that authenticity included moments of imperfection. Self-compassion allowed me to honor my own humanity, to accept that growth was a process rather than a destination. This approach helped me create a life that felt whole and fulfilling, a life that honored both my strengths and my vulnerabilities.

Living authentically also meant allowing myself to find joy in simplicity. As I embraced my true self, I realized that I did not need to seek validation through external achievements or approval. Instead, I found fulfillment in the small moments, in the quiet joys of daily life. This simplicity became a source of peace, a reminder that authenticity was about finding contentment within rather than chasing it in the world around me. By focusing on what truly mattered, I was able to create a life that felt rich and meaningful, a life that reflected my inner values.

Through this journey, I learned that authenticity required me to let go of comparison. For so long, I had looked to others to define my worth, to measure my progress against someone else's journey. But as I embraced authenticity, I understood that my path was unique, that I could create a life that was true to who I was without needing to conform to others' expectations. Letting go of comparison allowed me to find joy in my own journey, to appreciate my growth without the pressure to keep up with anyone else. This freedom became a foundation for my life, a reminder that I could live with peace and contentment, knowing that my journey was enough.

Reflecting on this journey, I felt immense gratitude for the gift of authenticity. Living authentically had allowed me to release the need for perfection, to embrace life as it was rather than as I thought it should be. By choosing to live in alignment with my own values and truth, I was able to create a life that felt whole, a life that reflected both my journey and the person I was becoming. This authenticity became a foundation for each new experience, a reminder that I could face the future with confidence and joy.

As I moved forward, I carried this authenticity with me as a source of strength and peace. Living authentically allowed me to approach life with a heart that was open, a spirit that was unburdened, and a sense of purpose that was true to who I was. By embracing authenticity, I had created a life that felt rich, meaningful, and true—a life that honored both my growth and my resilience.

Foundations for Embracing Authenticity and Inner Peace

1. **Embrace Growth as an Ongoing Journey**: Allow yourself the freedom to evolve. Growth supports authenticity by helping you align with your evolving self.

2. **Practice Self-Compassion in Moments of Doubt**: Approach yourself with kindness. Self-compassion allows you to live authentically, honoring both strengths and imperfections.

3. **Find Joy in Simplicity and Release Comparison**: Focus on what truly matters. Simplicity and

freedom from comparison support a life of peace and inner fulfillment.

As I continued to embrace authenticity, I found that living authentically also meant embracing a sense of purpose. The purpose was not about grand achievements or external accomplishments; it was about aligning my actions with the values I held dear. Each day, I sought to engage in actions that felt meaningful, to contribute to the world in ways that honored my true self. This sense of purpose gave me a reason to move forward, a sense of direction that allowed me to approach each day with intention and clarity.

One of the most powerful aspects of living authentically was the freedom to be present. When I let go of the need for external validation, I found that I could engage with each moment more fully, without the distractions of comparison or self-doubt. This presence allowed me to connect with others in meaningful ways, to experience life's joys and challenges with a heart that was open and receptive. By being present, I was able to live a life that felt whole, a life that reflected my commitment to authenticity and growth.

Living authentically also meant embracing change. There were times when I had clung to familiar patterns or relationships, fearing that change would disrupt my sense of self. But as I deepened my commitment to authenticity, I understood that change was a natural part of growth, an opportunity to evolve in alignment with my values.

147

Embracing change allowed me to approach life with flexibility and resilience, to trust that I could adapt while still staying true to who I was. This openness to change became a source of strength, a reminder that authenticity was not about staying the same but about evolving with grace.

In this journey, I found that living authentically required courage. There were times when authenticity meant standing up for myself, moments when it required me to honor my own needs even when it was difficult. This courage allowed me to engage with life from a place of integrity, to build relationships that were grounded in mutual respect and understanding. By choosing courage, I was able to create a life that felt true to who I was, a life that reflected my commitment to living authentically, no matter the challenges.

Reflecting on this journey, I felt a deep sense of gratitude for the freedom that authenticity had brought into my life. Living authentically had allowed me to release the expectations of others, to engage with life from a place of peace and joy. This authenticity had become a foundation for everything else—a way of living that allowed me to face each day with hope, resilience, and a heart that was open to the beauty of each moment.

As I moved forward, I carried this authenticity with me, a reminder that I could approach life with courage, peace, and purpose. Living authentically allowed me to create a life that felt rich and meaningful, a life that honored both my growth and the values I held dear. By embracing authenticity, I had created a life that felt true, a life that reflected both my journey and the strength I had found within myself.

Guiding Principles for a Purposeful and Authentic Life

1. **Align Actions with Purpose and Values**: Engage in meaningful actions that honor your true self. Purpose gives direction to authenticity, allowing you to live with intention.

2. **Embrace Presence to Experience Life Fully**: Let go of distractions and engage with each moment. Presence supports authenticity by allowing you to live without comparison or self-doubt.

3. **Approach Change with Openness and Courage**: Trust in your ability to adapt. Change is part of growth, supporting a life that evolves in alignment with authenticity.

As I continued to reflect on what it meant to live authentically, authenticity also involved honoring my emotional well-being. Living authentically meant allowing myself to feel the full range of emotions, embracing both the joys and the challenges of life without judgment. This approach allowed me to engage with my emotions as they were, to find wisdom in each feeling without labeling them as "good" or "bad." By honoring my emotions, I was able to live with a heart that was open and unburdened, a heart that approached each moment with acceptance.

In this journey, I discovered the importance of creating space for solitude. There were moments when I needed time alone, times when I needed to step back from the noise of the world to connect with myself. Solitude allowed me to reflect on my own needs and desires, to tune into the quiet voice within. This time for self-reflection became essential to living authentically, a way of reconnecting with my own values and purpose. By allowing myself space for solitude, I was able to navigate life with a sense of clarity and calm.

Living authentically also required me to let go of perfectionism. For so long, I needed to be perfect to be accepted or loved. But as I embraced authenticity, I understood that perfectionism was a barrier to my true self, a mask that kept me from fully engaging with life. Letting go of perfectionism allowed me to embrace my imperfections, to approach each moment with a sense of freedom and self-acceptance. This shift allowed me to create a life that felt rich and fulfilling, a life that celebrated my humanity.

Through this journey, I learned that living authentically was also about finding balance. There were times when I needed to push myself, moments when growth required effort and resilience. And then there were times when I needed to rest, to honor my own limits and recharge. By finding a balance between growth and rest, I was able to create a life that felt sustainable and nourishing. This balance became a foundation for everything else, a reminder that authenticity was not about pushing myself endlessly but about respecting my own pace and needs.

Reflecting on this journey, I felt immense gratitude for the freedom and peace that authenticity had brought into my life. Living authentically allowed me to approach each day with a sense of purpose, to engage with the world from a place of integrity and strength. This authenticity became a foundation for each new experience, a way of living that allowed me to navigate life with confidence, compassion, and a heart that was open to the beauty of each moment.

As I moved forward, I carried this authenticity with me, a reminder that I could approach life with hope, courage, and an unwavering commitment to my own well-being. Living authentically had given me the freedom to create a life that felt true, a life that honored both my growth and my resilience. By choosing authenticity, I had created a life that felt rich, meaningful, and whole—a life that reflected both my journey and the values I held dear.

▌ Foundational Practices for Authentic Living

1. **Honor Your Emotions Without Judgment:** Embrace your feelings as they arise. Emotional acceptance supports authenticity by allowing you to live with a heart that is open and unburdened.

2. **Create Space for Solitude and Self-Reflection:** Take time to connect with yourself. Solitude allows you to tune into your own values, needs, and desires.

3. **Let Go of Perfectionism for True Freedom:** Release the need to be perfect. Letting go of perfectionism supports a life that celebrates your humanity and unique journey.

As I reached the final steps of this journey toward authenticity, I realized that authenticity was about creating a life of fulfillment, one that aligned with both my values and my aspirations. Living authentically was a commitment to show up each day as my true self, to engage with life in ways that felt meaningful. This approach allowed me to navigate the world with a heart that was open, unburdened, and ready to embrace both the joys and challenges of each new experience.

One of the most profound lessons I had learned was that living authentically was not about finding a final, perfect version of myself. It was about embracing my growth, honoring each phase of my journey, and understanding that I was always evolving. This acceptance allowed me to approach each day with patience and grace, to trust that authenticity was not a destination but a lifelong journey. By embracing this perspective, I was able to release the pressure to "arrive" and instead enjoy the richness of each moment.

In this journey, I also discovered that authenticity was deeply connected to self-love. Living authentically required me to treat myself with kindness, to honor my own needs and dreams without judgment. Self-love became a foundation for authenticity, a reminder that I was worthy of the peace and fulfillment I sought. This self-love allowed me to create a life that felt whole, a life that reflected both my strengths and my vulnerabilities. By choosing self-love, I was able to build a life that felt rich and meaningful, a life that celebrated my unique journey.

As I looked back on all that I had learned, I felt immense gratitude for the resilience, courage, and compassion that had guided me. This journey toward authenticity had transformed me in ways I had not anticipated, showing me the power of living in alignment with my true self. By embracing authenticity, I had created a life that felt rich, purposeful, and deeply fulfilling—a life that honored both my growth and my healing. Authenticity had become a foundation for everything else, a way of living that allowed me to approach each day with hope, confidence, and a heart that was open to the beauty of each new moment.

Reflecting on this journey, I felt a deep sense of peace. Living authentically had given me the freedom to engage with life in meaningful ways, to create relationships and experiences that felt true to who I was. This authenticity allowed me to live with integrity, to approach each new day with a spirit of resilience and joy. By choosing to live authentically, I had created a life that felt whole, a life that reflected both my journey and the strength I had found within myself.

As I moved forward, I carried this authenticity with me, a reminder that I could live each day with purpose, peace, and an unwavering commitment to my own well-being. Living authentically had given me the freedom to create a life that was rich and meaningful, a life that honored both my growth and the values I held dear. By choosing authenticity, I had embraced a life that felt true, a life that celebrated both my unique journey and the strength I had discovered along the way.

Final Reflections on Living Authentically

1. **Embrace Life as a Journey of Growth**: Allow yourself the freedom to evolve. Authenticity is a lifelong journey, not a destination.

2. **Cultivate Self-Love as a Foundation for Fulfillment**: Treat yourself with kindness. Self-love supports authenticity by allowing you to honor your own needs and dreams.

3. **Live Each Day with Purpose and Peace**: Approach life with a heart that is open and unburdened. Authenticity allows you to create a life that feels rich and meaningful, a life that reflects your true self.

Made in the USA
Las Vegas, NV
27 December 2024